Praise for Charles Strobel's
The Kingdom of the Poor

"In her foreword . . . Ann Patchett recalls that her friend's ordination card was printed with the words of Robert Kennedy: 'Few of us have the greatness to bend history itself, but each of us can work to change a small portion of events, and in the total of all those acts will be written the history of this generation.' That's just what Father Strobel did. Over the years, he managed to bring his congregation, and then his diocese, and then his whole city to an understanding of what we owe to our unhoused neighbors."

—MARGARET RENKL, *The New York Times*

"He put this together with his niece and a friend while he was dying, and it's a manual for how to be a decent person. . . . It's really such a beautiful and important book."

—ANN PATCHETT, on *The Today Show*

"Reading this posthumous memoir is a lot like experiencing Strobel in person. His stories welcome you into his life. He's always a little bit mischievous in his delivery. He is calm about his faults and mistakes in a way that is reassuring. . . . But what's most beautiful about this book is that it's not just about Charles Strobel. It's about the people who crossed his path as well. From the characters who challenged him to the folks who guided him in his daily thoughts and actions, the book sees Strobel through his lifelong experience in connecting with others."

—AMANDA HAGGARD, *Chapter 16*

"One might think that Father Strobel carried the weight of the world, or at least the unhoused world, on his back. That he was so troubled by a society ripe with seemingly insurmountable inequity and poverty at every turn that it kept him up at night. But no. The answer as to how—and in retrospect, the answer is the entire book—comes in the epilogue with another sentence. 'Take heart that if you do work that is for peace, you will be in communion. And if you are in communion, you will be at peace even in the presence of divine discontent.' *The Kingdom of the Poor* . . . is his story of how he came to be in communion every day of his life."

—JOE PAGETTA, *America Magazine*

"*The Kingdom of the Poor* is . . . a lifetime of stories illustrating Strobel's belief that 'we are all poor and we are all worthy of love.' His folksy stories are often amusing, yet memories of the segregated South, the example of family members who live to serve others, and folks who know how to 'make do' even when times are tough explain how Strobel's faith and character were formed."

—AMY PAGLIARELLA, *The Presbyterian Outlook*

"Want to be encouraged by selfless acts? *The Kingdom of the Poor*, by the late Father Charles Strobel—a revered figure in Nashville—his niece Katie Seigenthaler, and former Metro Nashville Schools board member Amy Frogge, is the true story of how Strobel started the Room In The Inn program for people who are unhoused."

—SARALEE TERRY WOODS, *Tennessee Lookout*

The Kingdom of the Poor

THE KINGDOM OF THE POOR

My Journey Home

CHARLES STROBEL

Edited by Katie Seigenthaler and Amy Frogge

Vanderbilt University Press | Nashville, Tennessee

Copyright 2024 Vanderbilt University Press
All rights reserved
First printing 2024
First paperback edition 2025

Library of Congress Cataloging-in-Publication Data
Names: Strobel, Charles F., 1943-2023, author. | Seigenthaler, Katie, editor.
Title: Kingdom of the poor : my journey home / Charles Strobel ; edited by Katie Seigenthaler and Amy Frogge.
Description: Nashville, Tennessee : Vanderbilt University Press, 2024. | Includes bibliographical references and index.
Identifiers: LCCN 2024016843 (print) | LCCN 2024016844 (ebook) | ISBN 9780826507365 (hardback) | ISBN 9780826507372 (epub) | ISBN 9780826507389 (pdf)
Subjects: LCSH: Strobel, Charles F., 1943-2023. | Catholic Church--United States--Clergy--Biography. | Priests--United States--Biography.
Classification: LCC BX4705.S8573 S77 2024 (print) | LCC BX4705.S8573 (ebook) | DDC 282.092 [B]--dc23/eng/20240609
LC record available at https://lccn.loc.gov/2024016843
LC ebook record available at https://lccn.loc.gov/2024016844

Front cover: Photo of Charles Strobel © George Walker IV – USA TODAY NETWORK via Imgn Images

Frontispiece: Father Charles Strobel, right, shares a moment with A. W. Forrest, left, Rondal Ferry, and John Monsue on the steps outside Room In The Inn. Nashville, TN, April 20, 1990. @ Mike DuBose—USA TODAY NETWORK

*For everyone who has struggled with life on the streets.
You are remembered. You are loved.*

CONTENTS

Foreword by Ann Patchett   ix
How The Kingdom of the Poor Came to Be:
  A Note from the Editors   xi
The Beatitudes   xvii

PROLOGUE. Why I Was Born   1

PART I. HOW MUCH IS ENOUGH?

CHAPTER 1. Mutt   5
CHAPTER 2. Sadie and Tony   10
CHAPTER 3. Horace Tidwell   17
CHAPTER 4. Clayton   21
CHAPTER 5. Mr. Orskiborsky   24

PART II. WORTHLESS SERVANTS

CHAPTER 6. Aunt Mollie and Aunt Kate   29
CHAPTER 7. Mr. Albert   34
CHAPTER 8. Mama   36

PART III. CHANGE YOUR WORLD

CHAPTER 9. Father Dan   43
CHAPTER 10. Prof Al   46
CHAPTER 11. The *Anawim*   49
CHAPTER 12. Ol' Grange   52
CHAPTER 13. Larry Munson   56
CHAPTER 14. Dr. Martin Luther King Jr.   60
CHAPTER 15. Myles Horton   67

PART IV. ROOM IN THE INN

CHAPTER 16. Mrs. Hopwood	75
CHAPTER 17. Lulabelle	77
CHAPTER 18. Michael "Bear" Hodges	80
CHAPTER 19. Madeleine DeMoss	85
CHAPTER 20. Gwen Benford	88
CHAPTER 21. Melvin Scates	90
CHAPTER 22. Rachel Hester	92

PART V. THE MIRACLE OF FORGIVENESS

CHAPTER 23. Billy Denton	97
CHAPTER 24. Antony and Cleopatra	100
CHAPTER 25. The Murderer	105
CHAPTER 26. The Japanese	110

PART VI. GETTING READY TO DIE

CHAPTER 27. The Pastor	117
CHAPTER 28. Vince	121
CHAPTER 29. The Man in the Morgue	127
CHAPTER 30. The Chaplain	132
EPILOGUE. Pick Up the Burden	139

Acknowledgments 147

Appendix A. Charles Strobel's Eulogy for His Mother, Mary Catherine Strobel *151*

Appendix B. Strobel Family Statement after the Murder of Mary Catherine Strobel *153*

Appendix C. Charles Strobel's Statement in Opposition to the Death Penalty for William Scott Day *155*

Appendix D. Room In The Inn Rights and Responsibilities *157*

Appendix E. Dr. Martin Luther King Jr.'s Principles of Nonviolence *159*

FOREWORD

Ann Patchett

A LONG TIME AGO, more than twenty years now, Charlie Strobel used to come to my house under the pretense of wanting editorial advice. He claimed to need my help making a speech shorter or an essay longer, when what he really wanted to do was sit on my couch and read to me. As a priest who devoted his life to serving the unhoused, Charlie spent his days patiently listening to other people, and I think he enjoyed a quiet audience every now and then. What's more, I was encouraging, always telling him I thought he should write a book. It was the only advice I ever gave but he showed no interest in taking it.

On one of those visits he gave me his ordination memorial card, dated January 31st, 1970, the day he became a priest. The card is on my desk now, printed with the famous words of Robert Kennedy, "Few of us have the greatness to bend history itself, but each of us can work to change a small portion of events, and in the total of all those acts will be written the history of this generation."

Through standing up for his ideals, and acting to improve the lot of others, and striking out against injustice, Charlie spent his life enacting Kennedy's words. I would even go so far as to say he bent history.

Years later, I wrote a piece about him for an anthology of saints. For several days, I followed him while he made his rounds, visiting the poor and the sick. When we returned to Room In The Inn, the magnificent campus for shelter and services for the unhoused he had founded, he gave me files of the things he had written and the things that had been written about him. We sat in a small conference room and I asked him questions about his life. Again and again, he told me how grateful he was for my interest. This time I had another idea: if he didn't want to write a book about himself, maybe I could write a book about him. The more stories I heard, the more stories I wanted him to tell me. But when he promised to think about it, he was only being polite. The answer was always no.

"They aren't making new Charlie Strobels," I told him. "When you're gone, we're going to need some sort of template to help us figure out how to do the things you're doing."

He would laugh. Charlie's laugh was its own sort of miracle, drenched in kindness and hilarity. We had the same conversation whenever we saw each other. "You or me or someone else," I would say. "This book needs to be written."

Writing about his own life's experiences, his beliefs and good work, might have felt in direct conflict with his humility and service to others. I would guess this was what held him back from the enterprise for so long. But as he neared the end of his life, he was too sick to help others, at least not in the ways he'd been helping them for so many years. The only gift he had left to give were his words, and so he gave them freely, with enormous love.

What you are holding is a manual for decency and kindness. The stories Charlie tells about his life are at once commonplace and astonishing. Did we ever live with this much acceptance and grace?

Did we at one time instinctively know how to seize the joy in baseball, in family, in service, before life's harsher voices threw us off course? Was there a time when we understood that all beings are connected, and did we soak up the tender relief that our connection ensures? *The Kingdom of the Poor* cuts through the noise of the world with a clear, bright note: *love, love, love*, it tells us. In reading this book, we remember who we are. We remember what matters. We remember the person that Charlie saw in us, in every one of us. At last we are standing as we were meant to stand: together.

HOW *THE KINGDOM OF THE POOR* CAME TO BE

A Note from the Editors

WE'D LIKE TO TAKE YOU BACK to the beginning of 2023, the eightieth and last year of Charles Strobel's remarkable life.

Parkinson's disease and diabetes were taking him down. The man known as Father Strobel to those he served, Charles to his family, and Charlie to his many friends, was losing weight, losing his mobility, losing his balance, losing his eyesight.

Those of us who loved him tried to think of ways we could help. We stopped by his apartment at Mary, Queen of Angels Assisted Living as often as we could. We played music and audiobooks for him. We read to him, talked with him, told him funny stories.

And we kept his television tuned, day and night, to baseball games. Baseball was the love of Charlie's life—and his metaphor for living a good one. He often said he'd play any position that got him on the field; he treated every at-bat as a chance to make a difference—to help his team move forward, to keep hope alive, to change the outcome. While he loved to play and participated in amateur leagues into his seventies, he gave himself wholly to the game even when he wasn't suited up. He coached whenever he could and was the consummate spectator, keeping meticulous stats from the stands. Charlie's way of approaching life and his way of approaching baseball were one and the same: each day, like each game, was a fresh opportunity to show up and do better.

In his final months, however, Charlie felt cut off from the field, from the dugout—even from the stands. A force of nature for justice, who used to be everywhere all at once, he was increasingly restless and frustrated within the confined spaces he was forced to occupy due to illness.

No amount of distraction could change the fact that Charlie was no longer fully immersed in the world of his family and his community. Especially painful to him was his separation from his family and community at Room In The Inn, the nonprofit Charlie founded in 1986 that has evolved over time into a national model for offering care, love, and hope to the unhoused.

Rachel Hester—executive director of Room In The Inn—realized her friend and mentor needed more than ways to pass the time. He needed a purpose.

Early in 2023, she asked Amy Frogge, her Room In The Inn colleague, to begin helping Charlie archive his immense catalogue of homilies, speeches, essays, and other writings. As Amy sat with him, day after day, reading his words back to him, she became aware that Charlie was shifting his focus from archiving to storytelling.

He began to envision a memoir. And his old spark returned. His body's limitations didn't seem to matter so much anymore. His mind began traveling far and wide, in communion with all the people who had touched his life and made him who he was. That famous smile, which had earned him the nickname "Sunshine" in high school, returned to his face. He was lit from within, on fire to tell his tales.

By March 2023, his niece Katie had joined Amy in serving as his scribe. We rushed to record his every word. We were racing against time. Charlie knew it and we knew it. He gave himself completely to the project the way he had given himself completely to everything he'd ever done. He asked us to put a sign on his door: "Please do not disturb from 2 to 4 p.m. I am writing." Always concerned about loving his neighbor, he thought for a moment and insisted we add, "I love you. —C. S."

Conspiratorially, he whispered to us, "Don't tell anyone what we're doing. I'm not ready to share it yet." Soon after he said this, a friend walked through his door. Charlie asked his friend to sit down next to him. Then he leaned in and, with a twinkle in his eye, said, "I'm writing a memoir. But don't tell anyone!"

Pretty soon, everyone who visited him was reading the pages of his memoir aloud to him and promising not to tell anyone else about it. Classic Father

Charlie Strobel sharing his memoir with caregiver Melanise Madlock.

Strobel. Classic Charles. Classic Charlie. Making rules for the sheer joy of breaking them.

Rules and laws annoyed Charlie. They always had. He felt they encouraged condemnation and shame. "Jesus didn't keep records," he liked to say. Instead, he was drawn to The Sermon on the Mount, which is introduced by the Beatitudes. Rather than laws that weigh us down, Charlie called the Beatitudes, "blessings that lift our spirits."

As he told us stories from every facet of his life, we began to realize they belonged together. Each one was a different expression of the Beatitude he held most dear: *Blessed are the poor, for theirs is the kingdom of heaven.* Each one illustrated, in some way, the cornerstone of his faith: we are all poor and we are all worthy of love.

Charlie was a relentless editor, constantly asking us to reread and modify the chapters he was constructing. One day, he said, "Let's read the part about the family in the horse barn again."

We read these words to him:

They lived behind the house next door to us in a horse barn that had been converted into a two-room tarpaper shack. I remember seeing the father get up at dawn every morning to work his day job delivering coal. He'd come home around six and after supper, he'd leave again to work as a janitor until midnight.

He did this six days a week but was never able to make enough money to get his family out of that horse barn and buy a real house. So as I was growing up and I heard people say that poor people were lazy and didn't want to work, I didn't see it that way. That was not my experience, not my frame of reference, at all.

Charlie raised his hand and held it still, indicating he wanted us to stop reading. He thought for a moment, then said, "For blessed are those we call poor. Their life is of the highest value." He asked us to add these words to the story of the family in the horse barn.

From then on, he composed simple prayers, which he called Beatitude Moments, to accompany every chapter:

Blessed are those who forgive. They shall find freedom, justice, and peace. Blessed are those who learn to live in mystery. They shall find delight. Blessed are those who accept limitations with grace. They shall rest in peace. And so on.

The last story Charlie told was about his godfather, Albert Eberhardt, a poor and gentle man who had lived down the street from the Strobel family's home in North Nashville and made a living as a carpenter. Mr. Albert embodied the attributes Charlie cherished the most: humility, generosity, and kindness.

On August 3, he finished encapsulating the life of Mr. Albert with this Beatitude Moment: *Blessed are those who choose to live humbly, for they shall lead by example.*

Over the next two days, Charlie continued to listen as people he loved—friends, family, and caregivers—read his stories to him. But he did not write any more.

Charles Frederick Strobel died peacefully on the morning of August 6, 2023, a Sunday.

He left us a vision of a better world. The pages of this memoir, whose creation consumed his final days, call each of us to keep building God's kingdom of justice and peace. The kingdom was very real to Charlie, existing everywhere the poor and lowly are exalted and celebrated.

He believed the place for celebration is around the communion table, breaking bread together, sharing a meal. It was the communion meal he savored every time his mother set a bowl of warm soup in front of him. It was the communion meal he served every time he handed someone a peanut butter and jelly sandwich. And it is the communion meal that has come to define the hospitality offered by Room In The Inn.

Communion is at the heart of the so-called simple stories Charlie dictated to us. In the inclusive spirit that was the hallmark of everything Charlie did, we also have included "Editors' Notes" throughout to supplement his memories with perspectives from family and friends.

Some of the stories in this book he was committing to the page for the first time. Some he revised or resurrected from his collected writings. All are about poor people, in body and spirit, who impacted him profoundly and convinced him we can reach the kingdom together.

We hope you savor reading *The Kingdom of the Poor*. We hope it gives you nourishment. We hope Charles Strobel's way in the world warms your heart, feeds your soul, and gives you strength to get out there and play.

Katie Seigenthaler and Amy Frogge

THE BEATITUDES

How blest are the poor in spirit; the reign of God is theirs.

Blest too are the sorrowing; they shall be consoled.

Blest are the lowly; they shall inherit the land.

Blest are they who hunger and thirst for holiness; they shall have their fill.

Blest are they who show mercy; mercy shall be theirs.

Blest are the single-hearted for they shall see God.

Blest too the peacemakers; they shall be called sons of God.

Blest are those persecuted for holiness' sake; the reign of God is theirs.

Blest are you when they insult you and persecute you and utter every kind of slander against you because of me.

Be glad and rejoice, for your reward is great in heaven.

Matthew 5: 3–10, New American Bible,
1970 St. Joseph Edition[*]

---

[*] Charles received a copy of The New American Bible in 1970, the year of his ordination to the priesthood. It became his most well-thumbed reference book and most reliable file folder, its pages crammed with funeral programs, holy cards, notes from friends, quotes he wanted to remember, and ideas for homilies or speeches he was working on. While he preferred to simplify the language of the Beatitudes when preaching and speaking, and wrote his Beatitude Moments using the word *blessed* rather than *blest*, he likely turned often to this version from Matthew 5: 3-10 in his New American Bible, 1970 St. Joseph Edition.

Charles—the name his family always called him—on his first birthday, March 12, 1944.

Charlie on his eightieth and last birthday, March 12, 2023. The banner behind him was a gift from his Room In The Inn community, whose members called him "Father Strobel."

Prologue

Why I Was Born

MARK TWAIN, THE GREAT AMERICAN FOLK HERO and writer, has said, "The two most important days of your life are the day you are born and the day you find out why."

The following pages help to explain why I was born.

They will include stories of growing up and the world I lived in that capture events, personalities, and experiences that shaped my life's work.

This is not meant to be a complete explanation of how difficult it was to live in a time full of painful memories—when racism and violence were common. It is not meant to be that.

It is a snapshot—a portrait, if you will—of a simple life, one that evolved through reflection on the Sermon on the Mount, which is introduced by the Beatitudes, the moral framework within which I have tried to live my life.

I believe every one of us has what I call Beatitude Moments—totally unexpected, grace-filled experiences when one is filled with love. We remember them as divine gifts from above—not simply memories. We are humbled when we receive such moments, such gifts, and we want to share them with people who understand.

This is why I have written this book—to share my Beatitude Moments with you: those blessings that cannot be proven and need not be argued about.

A Beatitude Moment is a grace-filled point and place in time that stays with you forever and is meant to be shared.

Before I even knew what the Beatitudes were, I experienced them as a small child who lived among the poor and the meek. Let me tell you about them. Let me tell you as well about how I came to understand the Beatitudes as a framework for living. Let me tell you why the Beatitudes continue to live in our midst. And let me tell you about the people who gave me a passion for loving the poor in body and spirit.

We are all poor and we are all worthy of love. This is the heart of my simple stories—each one a story of God.

PART I

How Much Is Enough?

1

Mutt

I ALWAYS WANTED TO KNOW my father better. Some of the sadness I carry is the sadness of not knowing him. I think it is a sadness borne of yearning. And I think he becomes a parable that reminds me of God the Father, both the positive aspects of being his son, and the yearning to see him and to know him even better.

Daddy's name was Martin. His nickname was Mutt. It was given to him because he was a hunchback. As a four-year-old, he fell from the top of a makeshift seesaw when the child at the bottom jumped off. His back slammed against a concrete curb and broke. Doctors were unsure how to treat him. They recommended hanging Daddy in suspension in the doorway of the family home, hoping the weight of his body would straighten out his spine. All this did was leave him in agony. His mother finally put a stop to it. With the help of his family, he learned to live with his affliction.

Daddy eventually became a dispatcher and secretary for the Nashville Fire Department and everyone there loved him. He died suddenly of a heart attack in December 1947. He was only forty-six. Early in 1948, the firemen asked the fire chief, "Would you give his wife the job of secretary?" His wife was my mother, Mary Catherine Schweiss Strobel. We called her Mama.

Sure enough, the chief gave Mama the job. She was thirty-five years old and the mother of four young children. She became the first female employee of the fire department. She worked there for the next twenty-nine years and was the only woman in the department for the first twelve of those years.

Mama told some interesting stories about Daddy over the years. She recalled their courtship, during which he wrote her this poem on Valentine's Day, 1936:

> I cannot read a word of Greek
> And only English do I speak.
> There is in all my pedigree
> No trace of Mayflower ancestry.
> My search for wealth has been in vain.
> Too well I know that I am plain—
> I've led a sketchy life—'tis true
> And tho unfit to tie your shoe,
> My dreams are made of sturdy stuff
> And I love you. Is that enough?

Mama also told us she waited a number of years before deciding to marry Daddy. I asked, "Mama, why did you take so long?" She said, "I wish I hadn't waited. I always wanted to have a dozen children."

"Well, what kept you from it? I mean, y'all were dating."

"No, no, no, we weren't dating. He just picked me up and drove me to places."

"So, he was your chauffeur?"

"Well, I guess he was."

"Well, that's a date."

"No, it wasn't a date. Don't go talking that way."

She added, "I loved him to death, but I heard some of the relatives say, 'I wonder what the children will look like.'"

Mama meant that her family was concerned their children would be born crippled. I responded that this sounded archaic and asked why she didn't consult a doctor. She said, "Well, I didn't know what to do, but I worried and worried. Isn't that amazing? But that was 1935. That was the way people thought. And I guess you all turned out all right!"

I remember Daddy coming home at 11 p.m. from a night shift and getting up to work the 7 a.m. shift. On other occasions, I recall waking up to the smell of bacon and eggs and biscuits and running to jump in his lap to eat breakfast. I

Martin Strobel, whose back was broken in a childhood accident, with his children Jerry, Veronica, and Charles on Father's Day, 1947.

also went with him when the pastor at our parish church, Father Aaron T. Gildea, had to make a communion call, go to the hospital, or to the nursing home. Father Gildea could not drive, so Daddy drove him to all these places of care. I was in the backseat bouncing around and feeling really close to him.

Some of my fondest memories of Daddy are what I call "fun and games." After a long night of work, he wanted to do two things—read the morning paper and play with his little boy. But the little boy was keeping him from reading the paper. So he said, "Let's play barbershop." I put a sheet around him, walked around his head, and pretended to be a barber cutting his hair. He got to drink his coffee and read the paper, I got to cut his hair, and it worked.

Daddy came from a family of musicians. He was a classical pianist who loved to play Rachmaninoff. While he lived, our house was filled with music. But he did not live long enough.

I remember when he died. It was December 21, 1947, four days before Christmas. I was four-and-a-half years old.

Like all houses, ours was a buzz of activity as our family prepared for the holiday. But Daddy was not feeling well and was confined to bed.

When he died at midday, I remember Mama throwing up the bedroom window and screaming over and over again, "Call Father Gildea! Mutt just died!" Word spread quickly throughout the neighborhood. People started showing up, including Dr. Arthur Sutherland, my father's physician, and Father Gildea, our pastor at the Church of the Assumption.

By the end of the day, our house was full of family and friends, stopping by to mourn with us. Before long, it was hard to move. What I remember about the house being full, from my perspective as a small boy, was of being in a sea of adults but only seeing them from the knees down.

My Aunt Mary Glaser, my father's sister, drove Mama and me to Martin's Funeral Home, where Daddy had been taken after he died. Mama wanted to go alone, but I insisted that I wanted to see what was happening.

When we got to Martin's, Mr. Martin escorted us upstairs to the room where Daddy lay a corpse on a double bed. Mama and Aunt Mary were there to pick out a casket and make arrangements for the funeral. Nobody had yet closed Daddy's eyes. I saw that they were wide open. My Aunt Mary walked over and gently closed them. We then picked out a casket that was made of pine and covered in light gray felt, a pauper's casket. It was not mahogany or metal, but humble, as it should have been.

Daddy's funeral Mass was on December 23, 1947, at the Church of the Assumption, which was located across the street and a few doors down from our house. His burial was at Calvary Cemetery, the place where Nashville Catholics were laid to rest.

> Blessed are those who face limitations with grace. They shall rest in peace.

EDITORS' NOTE: *Charles's younger sister Alice was four months old when their father died. Their sister Veronica was eight. Their brother Jerry was seven. Alice has no memories of her father and has always been fascinated by what her siblings, especially Charles, remember of him:*

Charles was so young when Daddy died, only four and a half. Yet his memories of their time together were surprisingly vivid, and he treasured them—the sweet ones and the sad ones.

Along with his heartbreaking visit to the funeral home with Mama, Charles also remembered reading his own name in Daddy's obituary.

2

Sadie and Tony

I WAS BORN IN NASHVILLE, TENNESSEE, on March 12, 1943, and grew up north of the Bicentennial Mall, a block off Jefferson Street. Our two-bedroom house was located at 1212 Seventh Avenue North. We loved it and had a name for it: "Twelve-Twelve." It was down the street from our parish church and school, the Church of the Assumption. We called it "the Assumption" or "Assumption" and it was our second home.

I remember scenes when I was five or six years of age that stick with me today and have so much to do with my formation.

Daddy died when I was four, leaving Mama to raise four children. The oldest, my sister Veronica, was not yet nine at the time. Mama also was responsible for her two elderly aunts, Aunt Mollie and Aunt Kate, who lived with us. This meant that Mama had to work outside the home to put food on our table.

As I have mentioned, Daddy had been a dispatcher for the Nashville Fire Department and, later, a secretary. The chief of the department offered Mama Daddy's secretarial job. She took it. She made $185 a month. Aunt Mollie and Aunt Kate, who were eighty and seventy-eight when Daddy died, took care of us during the day while Mama went to work.

North Nashville was known at that time as Cab Holler, not Germantown. It was like other poor parts of the city with quirky names like Varmint Town, Flatrock, Rock City, and Trimble Bottom.

Two blocks away from our house, across from Werthan Bag Company, was Cheatham Place, one of the city's first public housing developments. Built by the federal government, Cheatham was a step up for people who had been living in houses with outhouses in the back. Cheatham was for White families only. Andrew Jackson Courts was built in Nashville's Black community, which was also near where we lived but segregated from the rest of the city. Both Cheatham Place and Andrew Jackson Courts were called "the projects."

Although some folks rode buses to the western part of town to do domestic work, most folks worked in the area—and everyone was poor.

In the economy of the time, the poor worked for the poor. And they found dignity in the work. People grew vegetables and sold them off the backs of horse-drawn wagons. Men sold blocks of ice for what were called "ice boxes," not refrigerators. Others hauled coal to burn. Men with wagons picked up people's food garbage and fed it to their pigs. They were known as the "slop men." Other people "took in laundry," as the expression went. They were the washer women in the neighborhood since they were the only ones with washing machines.

Miss Poole was our washer woman. Even though she did our laundry, our clothes still needed ironing. In our house that was one of many chores, along with cooking and cleaning, that Aunt Mollie and Aunt Kate handled. My aunts were old women and Mama tried to lessen their load by hiring a woman named Sadie to help with the ironing. Sadie, too, was old, in her seventies. But there was no such thing then as being on a "fixed income." Sadie's only income was what she made cleaning and ironing. She was African American.

Once a week, Sadie would come to do the ironing for a few hours. She always stayed for lunch. But she never ate at the main kitchen table. She ate at the side table. I can remember asking her to eat at the main table with us, but she always politely declined.

What sticks with me most are the conversations she and I had about this. I would say, "Miss Sadie, why don't you eat at the big table with us?" Sadie would say, "No thank you, Mistah Charles, I'll just eat here by the window. It's cooler."

When I responded with, "Miss Sadie, you don't have to call me 'Mistah Charles.' Nobody calls me that," Sadie would say, "OK, Mistah Charles."

Every time I asked her not to call me "Mistah Charles," she would answer, "OK, Mistah Charles." I was a six- or seven-year-old child.

All of us now know of the centuries of segregation expressed in so many forms of hatred, violence, and death that denigrated generations of people of color from the time they were first enslaved and brought to America in 1619. Sadie and her ancestors experienced such denigration. Their race only compounded their poverty.

But I was too young to know what caused Sadie to call me "Mistah Charles." Or the risk she could not take, even in the safety of our home, to eat at the main table.

We were an apartheid culture back then—that's just the way it was. And there was no great movement to want to change that. Not even among the churches.

I remember meeting Tony Winston on the Assumption School playground. Again, I was about six or seven. Tony and his family lived one block over from us on Sixth Avenue North where Monell's restaurant is now. They were African American. Tony told me he was Catholic, and I asked him where he went to school. He said he went to St. Vincent's, which was out by Fisk University, a historically Black college. I asked him why he didn't go to Assumption with me; it was closer to his house. He just said, "Because I go to St. Vincent's."

I went home and told Mama I met a boy on the playground named Tony who was Catholic. She said, "Oh, the Winstons are such a nice family." I asked her why he didn't go to school with me, and she simply said, "Because he goes to St. Vincent's." I remember thinking that this didn't make sense and wasn't right.

Later, I would come to understand two evils were at work: that one hundred years after the Civil War, racial segregation was legal, and that more churches didn't take the lead in ending it.

EDITORS' NOTE: *Monsignor Owen Campion, a priest of the Nashville Catholic Diocese and Charles's close friend, tells the story of desegregation at Father Ryan High School, the all-boys Catholic high school he and Charles attended in the 1950s:**

In 1954, soon after the Supreme Court's landmark decision in *Brown vs. Topeka Board of Education* outlawed segregation in public schools, Father Ryan began accepting Black students. It was one of the first schools in the former Confederacy to integrate. It was so novel for a school to integrate at that time that one of the national broadcast networks came to Nashville to report the story. Father Francis Shea was the principal at the time and the reporter asked him how many Black students were enrolled at Ryan. Father Shea responded that he didn't have any idea because the school didn't count students by race.

The decision by the Diocese of Nashville was very contentious among the Nashville population. For a time, Catholic police officers on the Nashville force organized themselves during their off hours to protect the Nashville Bishop, William Adrian. I was a freshman at Father Ryan that year and I remember my mother being terrified the school might be bombed. Still my parents never considered removing me from Ryan.

Charles was a few years younger than I was. By the time he was a student at Father Ryan, Father James Hitchcock was the principal. The Nashville Interscholastic League (NIL), which was the athletic association presiding over all high school sports, notified Father Hitchcock that if Father Ryan allowed any Black players on its teams, the school would be kicked out of the NIL. Father Hitchcock stated that under no circumstances would Black students be removed from the school's teams and that if Ryan were expelled from the NIL, its sports programs would be intramural only.

These actions by priests at Father Ryan made such a big impression on Charles and me and on many other students, setting an example for us of the role of the Church in speaking out against injustice.

* Msgr. Campion was editor of the *Tennessee Register*, the state's Catholic newspaper, from 1971 to 1988 before accepting a position as the associate publisher of *Our Sunday Visitor*, the national Catholic weekly headquartered in Huntington, Indiana.

As a child, very little of the turmoil going on in the outside world with respect to injustice penetrated my safe and secure bubble.

I remember a lot of fun and games in our neighborhood, including a fair amount of mischief. For instance, one Sunday morning in September of 1957 when I was fourteen, the doorbell rang as we were getting ready for church. I went to the door and saw a man sprawled out on the porch. I assumed he was one of the homeless men—we called them "hobos" back then—who frequently knocked on our door, knowing Mama would always find something to give them. I hollered out to Mama, "There's a man on the porch looking for something to eat!" She called back, "Go fix him a sandwich!"

I went to the kitchen to make the man a sandwich. When I got back to the front door, two of my cousins jumped out of the bushes and cried, "Surprise! Surprise! We fooled you!" They had taken some old clothes and stitched them together to create a "dummy" that looked remarkably like a real man.

This led to a whole day of pranks. We schemed a plan to use the dummy to play tricks on unsuspecting people. Mama told us, "You'd better not. Somebody's going to call the police." We protested we'd be okay, and then headed out, ready to wreak havoc. First, we threw the dummy at passing cars, then hid and laughed as panicky people jumped out and ran over to see who they'd hit.

Next, we got the bright idea to climb to the roof of the Buddeke House with the dummy. The Buddeke House was right across the street from the Assumption and had been one of the most stately mansions in North Nashville back when Germantown was prosperous. After the Buddeke family moved away from Germantown, their home came to be used by the Assumption. It was the hub for all kinds of parish activities, including dances, bingo games, and parish suppers. We called it the Club House, and neighborhood kids like me used to organize games like baseball, basketball, Red Rover, hide and seek, and capture the flag in what was known as "the Club Yard" surrounding the house. We played there until our parents called us to supper.

The day my cousins made the dummy, we took it to the roof of the Buddeke House and started to wrestle with it, pretending like we were fighting. We waited until a bus approached and threw the dummy off the roof. It bounced on the concrete below. The bus driver stopped his bus, and all the passengers got out to help the poor man who had been thrown from the Buddeke House roof.

During all the ruckus, something told me I'd better go home. I slipped away just in the nick of time; somebody did call the police, as Mama predicted. They took my cousins down to juvenile court and kept them overnight before releasing them the following morning.

I remember feeling such relief I had not gotten caught but wondering why anyone would call the police just because we were pulling pranks with a dummy. What I didn't know was that the police, my neighborhood, and the whole city were on edge. Racial unrest was beginning to roil Nashville. Pro-segregationists had bombed a local school, Hattie Cotton Elementary School, on September 10, 1957—not long before our adventures with the dummy—because the school had dared to integrate the day before.

Hattie Cotton Elementary, located in East Nashville just across the river from our North Nashville neighborhood, was one of the first public schools in the city to finally open its doors to Black children. Following the Supreme Court's *Brown vs Topeka Board of Education* decision in 1954, which ruled that state laws establishing segregated schools were unconstitutional, Nashville adopted a plan to begin integrating its public schools one grade level at a time. The process began on September 9, 1957, when nineteen Black six-year-olds attempted to attend six all-White Nashville elementary schools. Hattie Cotton admitted a single Black student named Patricia Watson. Racist members of the community drove by schools that day, intimidating and threatening Black families and spitting on and cursing Black first-graders.

Just after midnight following that first day of school, dynamite exploded at Hattie Cotton, blowing a hole in the building, and causing extensive damage. No one was hurt, but the bombing ignited justified rage within the Black community. A segregationist and Ku Klux Klan member named John Kasper was questioned in connection with the crime. Although he was never charged with the bombing, nor was anyone else, Kasper was convicted one year later of having incited rioting after publicly vowing, just before Hattie Cotton blew up, that "blood will run in the streets of Nashville before Negro children go to school with whites."

The bombing of Hattie Cotton was a catalyst for the Nashville Student Movement, which was initiated among students at Nashville's historically Black colleges and universities (HBCUs) by Reverend James Lawson. In the late 1950s and early 1960s, he held workshops in nonviolent protest of racial segregation. These lessons in responding to hatred and violence with love and nonviolence would eventually lead to the famous Nashville lunch counter sit-ins of the early 1960s that ultimately desegregated many of the city's public institutions and establishments. The leaders of the Nashville Student Movement, such as James Bevel, Bernard Lafeyette, John Lewis, and Diane Nash, would eventually become nationally prominent Civil Rights leaders.

By the time the Nashville Student Movement was gaining momentum, I was also a college student, finally awakening to the wider world beyond my little corner of Nashville and giving a name to the wrongs I witnessed as a child in the presence of Sadie and Tony: racism. I was coming to recognize the existence of other kinds of poverty: poverties of equal rights and justice suffered by Black people, and poverties of fairness and humanity suffered by those who oppress them.

I would become deeply drawn to the examples of nonviolent resistance as practiced by the leaders and participants in America's Civil Rights Movement and would try to apply these practices to every type of poverty I encountered for the rest of my life.

> Blessed are they who endure bigotry and hatred, for the long arc of justice will one day bend their way.

3

Horace Tidwell

MAMA USED TO TELL the story that before Daddy got his job as a dispatcher with the fire department, he worked in a small grocery store in Cab Holler. Rather than tend the store, Daddy preferred to play baseball in the field across the street from it. He'd organize games with the guys in the neighborhood, and when a customer came in to buy some bread or milk, he'd cry out to them from the field, "Just put your money on the counter!" while he continued to play.

Daddy was athletic, despite his broken back, and he followed all sports. He loved boxing; his favorite boxer was Joe Louis, the Brown Bomber. He also loved football and tried to talk Mama into naming my older brother Jerry "Knute" after the legendary Notre Dame football coach Knute Rockne. But his favorite sport was baseball, and his favorite team was the New York Yankees. I wanted to be like him in every way, so it became my favorite sport, too, and I was thrilled to hear Mama say I was like Daddy in our shared love of the game.

My brother Jerry was as big a baseball fanatic as I was. From the time we were strong enough to lift a bat, we played every chance we got. There was no official youth baseball back then. Little League had not yet come to Nashville. So, we organized our own teams from the neighborhood.

Our field was either our backyard or the Club Yard up the street. Our bases were old cardboard squares. The grass surrendered each summer to our running, stealing, sliding, and digging into bat. Within weeks, the yard was pure dirt and the dirt was ground deep in our jeans, a chore for Aunt Mollie and Aunt Kate to scrub away at the end of the day.

Jerry and I were always competitive, and that extended to baseball. My hero was Stan "The Man" Musial of the St. Louis Cardinals; Jerry's was Ted "Teddy Ballgame" Williams of the Red Sox. Up and out of bed each morning, we raced to the front stoop to get the paper, and wrestled for the sports pages to see which player had the higher batting average in the previous night's game.

Then one summer night in 1953, when I was ten years old, baseball took on a whole new presence and meaning in my life.

EDITORS' NOTE: *Charles and Jerry Strobel shared an unbreakable bond of brotherhood and baseball. Jerry offers this remembrance:*

I think all kids like to pick a favorite player. I picked Ted Williams, the last man to bat .400 in a single season. He was also a remarkable man. He was a pilot in World War II and in the Korean War and he worked hard to get Black ballplayers into the majors. He was a champion for fairness, just a tremendous, tremendous person.

Charles picked Stan Musial, who was quite a baseball player, too—although of course I thought Williams was better! Musial had the same number of hits on the road as he did at home. He also played the harmonica. He'd play before games in the clubhouse.

Charles sure picked a good one in Stan The Man.

Strobel family friend and baseball fan Horace Tidwell with Mary Catherine and her children in the summer of 1948.

We had just spent the evening with Mama's good friend Bernice Tidwell and her husband Horace, who often invited us to an early supper on summer evenings.

Mama did not drive in those days; she had always relied on Daddy for transportation. Horace would come to our house to pick us all up and then take us home again. Horace was a gregarious, friendly, red-faced train engineer who loved to tell stories.

That particular night, on the drive home after supper, the car was packed with Mama, Aunt Mollie, Aunt Kate, Veronica, Jerry, Alice, and me. We were all listening and laughing along with Horace's stories.

But then I heard sounds coming from Horace's radio—wonderful sounds, mesmerizing sounds. I didn't know what they were, but I needed to know. I did something I had been taught never to do and—as a shy child, who didn't talk very much—had never done before: I interrupted Horace's story.

"Horace, what is that?" I blurted out.

"That's the Nashville Vols playing baseball," he said, naming the city's minor-league team. "They're playing Mobile tonight at Sulphur Dell, just off Jefferson Street."

"And they're on the radio?"

"Yeah, they broadcast all the games," he said. "Sometimes, on a good night, I can hear them on the train all the way from Chattanooga. But it's kind of hard to listen over the noise of that diesel engine."

"Who's the announcer?"

"Larry Munson," said Horace. "He's a legend. The best there is."

"What station are they on?"

"WKDA," he said.

My questions kept coming. "What time do they come on?" "Who are the teams they play?" "Are they in first place?" "Who are the players?" "Who's the manager?"

By that time, we were almost home, heading over the Jefferson Street Bridge. It was then that I saw one of the most beautiful sites I'd ever seen because I finally recognized it for what it was: there in the moonlit night, across the Cumberland River, were the bright lights of Sulphur Dell.

It was thrilling to hear the sounds of the radio inside the car, knowing it all was happening in that ballpark just a few blocks away. When we reached home,

I rushed into the house, ran to our radio in the front hall, and twisted the dial to find Larry Munson and the Vols for the first time.

That radio always gave us trouble because it was rather old. It was one of those Motorola models, standing about sixteen inches high and twelve inches wide, rounded at the top, covered in a brown veneer finish with a cloth speaker imbedded in its base and a little lighted dial in the center. There were only two knobs. One was the on/off and volume control knob; the other rotated the station numbers in the one-inch dial that was illuminated with a yellow light. From then on, I made sure it was set to AM 1240 WKDA.

I don't remember who won the game that night. I'd like to think Nashville did. But it didn't really matter. I was in love.

> Blessed are they who shine their light, for they will show others how to see.

4

Clayton

THE RAGS-TO-RICHES MAN is an American folk hero. But as much as we like to think of ourselves as self-made by our own initiative and determination, our bootstraps mentality is a myth. We have received throughout our lives wonderful gifts of love and support from so many generous people. Often these people appear on our journey to care for us when we are most in need.

Since I was a boy, I have always been sad about the inequalities I saw all around me, which were based on economic theories and social mores that never made sense to me as part of any true moral framework. Ironically, it has also been my experience that the poor return our stinginess with great warmth and generosity.

When I was around twelve years old, my friends and I would go out at night on our bikes with our pockets filled with firecrackers. We'd ride down to a weedy piece of land at Seventh Avenue North south of Jefferson Street that was known as "The Jungle." A bunch of homeless men would camp out there, huddled around their oil-can fire.

We were young and stupid and thought it was funny to race past them on our bikes and fling firecrackers at them before racing off. After doing it a couple of times, though, we started to feel bad about it. So one night, we came in a little closer and got to talking with them.

Their self-appointed leader was a man named Clayton Massie. He and his friends had nothing—but they invited us to share their campfire even though we'd been unkind to them. While they mixed their formula of Upper Ten [soda] and Soilox [fertilizer], they told us their stories full of life and love and laughter, but also tragedy and grief, broken promises, forgotten dreams, and lost hopes.

I became attached to them and kept coming back. They always treated me kindly as their younger brother or son. Long before I ever took the homeless in, they took me in and taught me how I should treat everyone, how I should be kind to everyone.

> Blessed are they who provide hospitality,
> for they shall know God's love.

The Church of the Assumption on Seventh Avenue North.

EDITORS' NOTE: *Charles once described Clayton to his niece Katie Seigenthaler as, "an old banty rooster kind of a fella," and recalled Clayton saying, "I'm an Irish Catholic and I'd be in the major leagues today if I hadn't gotten shot in the legs when I was in the Marines."*

Charles said he learned a lot about hospitality, not just from Clayton, but from the way others treated Clayton. Charles shared with her these two stories several years before he died. One of them involves Father Dan Richardson, the pastor of the Assumption and a huge influence in Charles's life:

Most of the cops in North Nashville were good guys, but there was one sergeant with a mean streak. I remember one day Clayton and a couple of other homeless men were just hanging out on Seventh Avenue North, and here came this sergeant and he started kicking them and hitting them with a billy club. He stood over Clayton and yelled, "Massie get up!" Clayton couldn't get up. So the sergeant picked him up and threw him in the paddy wagon and his head slammed against the back wall. I can hear and feel his head slamming against that back wall to this day. There was no reason for it. I never forgot it.

I also remember Father Dan hearing confessions before Midnight Mass on Christmas Eve one year. Clayton was in the back of the church, hustling people as they came in. He had a big old hat, and he laid it down somewhere. Then he panhandled enough to get himself through the night and wanted to leave. But he couldn't find his hat.

He started walking around the church yelling, "Where's my hat!? Where's my goddamn hat?!" People were deeply offended by the way Clayton was disrupting the solemnity of the church, but nobody knew what to do.

Finally, Father Dan exploded out of the confessional and bellowed, "Somebody find Clayton's goddamn hat!"

… 5 …

Mr. Orskiborsky

ONE OF MY EARLIEST MEMORIES is of a man named George Orskiborsky.

Just about the time a child begins to explore the world beyond his own yard, I remember going down the street and into the Buddeke House alone for the first time. As I have mentioned, the Buddeke House was an old mansion that was used by the church for all kinds of purposes. I walked in and saw all these huge, ornate rooms with twelve-foot ceilings. I also saw a small room and discovered it was where the janitor lived. The janitor was George Orskiborsky.

I peeked inside this simple, single room. The only things I saw were a bed, table, hot plate, refrigerator, lamp, chair, radio, and some tools. I remember being excited and saying to myself, "That's enough. That's all I need." Then I remember thinking, "When I grow up, I want to be the janitor at the church."

> Blessed are they who live with little, for they shall know God's bounty.

I don't know if my visit to George Orskiborsky's room qualifies as the second most important day of my life—the day I learned why I was born. But it is close. It's the first time I remember thinking and wondering how much is enough.

That question undergirds so many of my experiences growing up. That question has never left me. It is at the heart of so many of my experiences.

I was raised in North Nashville, where the poor worked for the poor. That's how we got by. We took care of each other. And so everyone was basically content and happy. Our shared poverty drove us toward one another, not away.

What do I mean by our shared poverty? More than an economic condition, it's the awareness that we cannot be happy all by ourselves. This is our poverty, and all the riches in the world won't erase it.

I have always believed our real enemy is denying our shared poverty, which leads to a lack of understanding of and empathy for one another. That's what's driving this country and this world apart today.

What can bring us together?

I believe we come together when we embrace the poor, when we accept that we all start in the exact same place—the day of our birth. Each of us comes into this world blood-red, naked, weak, vulnerable, and dependent on others for survival. Everything else—from pigmentation to possessions to power to prestige—is irrelevant in the face of this shared poverty.

When we forget this basic truth, we end up fighting for our own survival rather than helping each other survive. We forget to be decent and kind.

> Blessed are those who know abundance and
> share it freely. They will have no regrets.

The Buddeke House, located across the street from the Assumption and a hub of parish life.

Even though I did not know Mr. Orskiborsky well, he had a major impact on the way I viewed the world. Another family on Seventh Avenue North also impacted my worldview even though I did not know them well.

They lived behind the house next door to us in a horse barn that had been converted into a two-room tarpaper shack. I remember seeing the father get up at dawn every morning to work his day job delivering coal. He'd come home around six and after supper, he'd leave again to work as a janitor until midnight. He did this six days a week but was never able to make enough money to get his family out of that horse barn and buy or rent a real house.

So as I was growing up and heard people say poor people were lazy and didn't want to work, that was not my experience, my frame of reference, at all.

> Blessed are those we call poor.
> Their life is of the highest value.

PART II
Worthless Servants

⋆ 6 ⋆

Aunt Mollie and Aunt Kate

Jesus said to his disciples: "Scandals will inevitably arise, but woe to him through whom they come. He would be better off thrown into the sea with a millstone around his neck than giving scandal to one of these little ones.

"Be on your guard. If your brother does wrong, correct him; if he repents, forgive him. If he sins against you seven times a day, and seven times a day turns back to you saying, 'I am sorry,' forgive him."

The apostles said to the Lord, "Increase our faith," and he answered: "If you had faith the size of a mustard seed, you could say to this sycamore, 'Be uprooted and transplanted into the sea,' and it would obey you.

"If one of you had a servant plowing or herding sheep and he came in from the fields, would you say to him, 'Come and sit down at table'? Would you not rather say, 'Prepare my supper. Put on your apron and wait on me while I eat and drink. You can eat and drink afterward'? Would he be grateful to the servant who was only carrying out his orders? It is quite the same with you who hear me. When you have done all you have been commanded to do, say, 'We are useless servants. We have done no more than our duty.'"

LUKE 17:1–10*

"USELESS SERVANTS." Depending on the biblical version, these words are also translated as "unworthy servants" or "undeserving servants" or, my personal favorite, "worthless servants." I don't know when or where it first dawned on me the truth of these words. I know I was already ordained a priest. I'm sure I'd

---

* From Charles's New American Bible, 1970 St. Joseph Edition.

read or heard the words before, but never thought about their full importance.

The "worthless servant" lesson is not the most easily recognizable in the Gospel. Most prefer the more popular lessons and parables of the Good Samaritan or the Prodigal Son or the Good Shepherd.

The "worthless servant" image is not a favorite text for preaching either. We prefer to remember Jesus saying, "I no longer call you servants for a servant doesn't know what his master is about, but I call you friends." In an age when we are drawn to messages about self-esteem, self-respect, self-love, and self-worth, hearing about being "worthless" isn't appealing.

For me, though, it is one of those tiny, golden nuggets hidden in the stream that unexpectedly appears while searching for a larger one. When I first heard it, it seemed so crystal clear to me. In a moment more intuitive than analytical, I experienced the truth of what it means to be called one who has no worth.

And I remember feeling this great sense of joy. I thought, "Oh, wouldn't it be great to live this way and have it on your tombstone: Worthless Servant!"

Since then, I've asked myself why an image that might strike others as abhorrent filled me with joy. I realized it was because of the joyful people I had known throughout my life who not only wanted to serve, but who loved and lived to serve.

Especially when I was a child.

When Daddy died, he left behind a household of seven: not only Mama, Veronica, Jerry, Alice, and me, but two of the most important people in my life—Aunt Mollie and Aunt Kate, who had lived with us since Mama and Daddy got married.

They were Mama's aunts—her father's sisters—and they had helped to raise Mama after her own mother died when she was just seventeen months old and an only child. Aunt Mollie was the older of the two sisters, small and thin and wiry. She moved around our house as if she came equipped with a battery that never drained. Aunt Mollie was always working—cooking, cleaning, hanging laundry, ironing, and tending to every single need we had. Aunt Kate was the younger sister. Though she was also very short—not much over four feet tall—she was as round as Aunt Mollie was thin. Aunt Mollie was widowed. Aunt Kate never married. In fact, she had entered the convent as a young girl, intent on becoming a Poor Clare nun and living a life of extreme poverty and constant prayer, closed off from the outside world. She ended up being far too sociable

Aunt Mollie with Jerry, baby Alice, Veronica, and Charles in the late summer or early fall of 1947, a few months before their father died.

Aunt Kate with baby Charles in the summer of 1943.

to endure the convent's long periods of silence. But I remember her praying constantly—and loudly—for everyone she knew.

Our house had two bedrooms. Aunt Kate and Aunt Mollie slept in the back bedroom while we slept in the front bedroom. I remember going into their room at the end of the day to kiss them goodnight and say prayers with them. Aunt Kate would sprinkle us with holy water. She doused us with so much holy water over the years she warped the floorboards around her bed.

Aunt Kate wasn't as physically active as Aunt Mollie. I remember that she loved to sit in her rocking chair on the porch and call out greetings to the neighbors, while I don't remember Aunt Mollie sitting much at all. But Aunt Kate's hands were always busy, and always on our behalf. I can see her in the kitchen chopping vegetables for soup. I can see her bent over her sewing, making us clothes or expertly patching the ones that were worn out in places.

Mostly, I remember that when Mama became a widow at age thirty-five and had to work outside the home for the first time in her life, Aunt Mollie and Aunt Kate told their grieving niece, whom they loved like their own child, not to worry. They would take care of everything, including and especially her little children. We were only nine, eight, five, and seven months of age. Aunt Mollie and Aunt Kate were eighty-one and seventy-nine. Yet they were the ones who gave Mama the courage to walk out the door.

My great aunts make the "worthless servant" image so powerful for me. Aunt Mollie and Aunt Kate were that way with us. For them, serving us was not a burden but a joy. They were worthless servants, which means we were their masters. They did everything they could for us, they never disciplined us, and I never remember them ever asking me to do anything for them or to help out around the house.

It probably explains how easy it was for me, later on, to believe Jesus' words, "I am among you as one who serves." The next step in logic is to believe the words of Psalm 121—that God loves us and provides for all our needs, just as any devoted servant would—because I had experienced this so lovingly from Aunt Mollie and Aunt Kate.

The genius of Aunt Mollie and Aunt Kate was their faith in the power of their loving service. It's said that a boy remains a boy until there's need for him to be a man. Aunt Mollie and Aunt Kate knew the time would come when I would have to serve. Gradually, over time, I remember cutting the grass and painting around the house to help out. Though I was praised for it, I remember more that I felt the pleasure of being of service.

Aunt Kate had health problems for many years and began to need more care than she was able to give. As my brother, sisters, and I grew older, we began to learn to be her servants, to try to care for her as lovingly as she had cared for us; we did so until she died at age eighty-eight in 1957.

Aunt Mollie began to slow down in her late eighties. She finally needed more care than she could give, too. As she became bedridden, Mama made sure Aunt Mollie stayed at home. For almost a decade, and while she continued to work full-time, Mama brought in loving caregivers to help with Aunt Mollie's round-the-clock care.

I will never forget the way Mama tended to the aunt who had sacrificed the middle and final decades of her life to make a motherless child feel less motherless and four fatherless children feel less fatherless. The child became the mother. The master became the servant. Aunt Mollie died peacefully at home in 1964 at the age of ninety-seven.

> Blessed are they who lovingly care for others.
> They shall be lovingly cared for.

7

Mr. Albert

I ALSO REMEMBER SOMEONE very important in my life who, had he heard himself described as a worthless servant, would have accepted the description without question.

His name was Albert Eberhardt and everyone in our neighborhood called him "Mr. Albert." Mr. Albert was my godfather.

Albert Eberhardt was a small, balding man, barely over five feet tall, with a slight frame and strong arms. He had gentle eyes, and his mouth was always turned into a slight smile. He and his brother Rudolph—everyone in the neighborhood called him "Mr. Rudolph"—lived in a little house just a few doors down from us on Seventh Avenue North, right across from the Assumption.

The brothers had been raised at St. Mary's orphanage and had never known their parents. After they became adults, they lived in a series of rooming houses around North Nashville but were forced to leave when they couldn't pay the rent. Father Dan Richardson, Assumption's pastor for most of the years I was growing up, bought a little house across from the church and let the Eberhardt brothers live there for next to nothing.

Mr. Rudolph was the devil-may-care younger brother, always looking for a fishing hole. Mr. Albert was the hard-working, responsible one, always looking out for his younger brother. In fact, Mr. Albert was a carpenter, like St. Joseph. He could fix anything, and people in the neighborhood made sure he made a living by paying him whatever they could to fix things around their houses that were broken.

Mr. Albert fixed a lot of things around our house, and Mama appreciated him so much. She also recognized that he needed a place at our table. He had an open invitation to Sunday dinner and to every major holiday, and he always took her up on the offer. He became part of our family, and he would often come in on a Sunday afternoon and head for the shelf where we kept all the puzzles. He loved to work them. My sister Alice and I loved to work them with him. He'd get one going at a card table in the living room and we'd play a game to see who could put in the last piece. Mr. Albert was quiet, but he had a competitive twinkle in his eye. He often won, but sometimes he'd make sure I got the last piece instead of Alice.

I used to wonder why Mama and Daddy chose Mr. Albert as my godfather. I came to believe it was because he was one of the best men they knew. In a neighborhood brimming with good people, Mr. Albert was regarded as the most spiritual of all. He never begged. He was a dignified man and never without a home, as poor as he was. I remember that he had little to give. But whatever money he had left after paying his bills, he gave to spiritual organizations that supported causes he cared about, like orphanages for Native American children.

Mr. Albert also never bragged about anything. He was possessed of that rarest of gifts: the inability to claim anything for himself. The worthless servant. My entire life, I understood how lucky I was that my parents chose the humblest man they knew to be my example of godliness.

> Blessed are they who choose to live humbly,
> for they shall lead by example.

Charles with his godfather Albert Eberhardt in 1967.

8

Mama

TO SERVE THE LORD is to become worthless—not because you have no worth, but because nothing you do or have, by comparison, is worth more than the gift of God's love. Who is worthy to merit such grace? As the centurion exclaimed in Matthew's gospel, "Lord, I am not worthy!"

Becoming a worthless servant only happens when the relationship is of love. Looking for rewards and thanks disappear from the equation altogether when love rules. "We've done no more than our duty" suddenly makes complete sense.

Mama sometimes used to say to us as children, "Ooooh, you're driving me crazy!" She didn't mean it literally, and we always understood that she was simply saying, in her way, that she was overwhelmed by our needs. Yet she never once ceased to meet them, no matter the obstacles standing in her way. She understood that we were her responsibility, and she accepted her responsibility with every ounce of love and energy she possessed. She embraced, in the way of all loving parents, her role as our servant—just as Aunt Mollie and Aunt Kate did.

Since I've never had children, it was not until I began to work with people who are homeless that I came to understand what it must have been like for all three of the women who raised me so well.

Each unhoused person I encounter is an individual, with a complex history and complex needs. Everyone who walks through my door has traveled their own long, excruciating journey—bearing a heavy burden of sorrow, pain, mistakes,

Charles as an infant with his mother, Mary Catherine, his brother, Jerry, and his sister Veronica.

abuse, and mental health struggles—to reach me. Sometimes I am overwhelmed by their needs. Sometimes, like Mama used to say of me, they drive me crazy! But I willingly accept my responsibility to be my brother's and my sister's keeper—my responsibility to serve without regard to what it may cost me.

Thinking of Mama, I once wrote a bit of verse about all the people without homes whom I had come to know:

> They present a million problems,
> but are not a problem.
> Is that what parents mean?

In the relationship of love that the scriptures call The Kingdom of God, generous and abundant service is not extraordinary. It is how things are. It's how people treat one another when they have faith in God's love and in each other.

Every kind of relationship that requires service from us—whether at work, school, home or in the neighborhood—has this same potential. But I would submit that we also have a moral obligation to enter into relationships with those who are outside the circle of our typical daily interactions—with those who have lost their mooring from the best of human society and its embrace.

In the biblical passage preceding the one about the worthless servant, Jesus tells his disciples how to treat one another: They are not to abuse the little ones; all the little people of the world. The weakest among us should not be stepped on or stepped over. And they are to forgive one another, even seven times a day.

The disciples are not ready to do this. They do not think they can carry it out; they feel ill-equipped for the journey, so they ask for more. "Increase our faith!" they say—a cry for help.

The same cry for help must be ours today. We occupy a world that constantly tells us to look out for ourselves first and try to get ahead. The world tells us revenge and retaliation are acceptable, that forgiving and looking out for others are unrealistic fantasies.

"Increase our faith!" We cry. Jesus says, "You have enough faith already." He tells us our small, mustard-seed faith is enough to uproot the mulberry tree and plant it where it's never been planted before. What we think will require extravagant effort is within our reach. We do not need more faith; we need confidence in the faith we have.

Mama's faith was a confident faith. She loved people, pure and simple. She treated everyone she met as if they were part of her family, and she was ready to serve them the way she would serve anyone she claimed as kin.

She was full of funny sayings, but there was always something in them that expressed her confidence everything would be alright if we just trusted in God and each other. One of my favorites was, "Put the big pot in the little pot!" This was Mama's practical manifestation of the Miracle of the Loaves and Fishes, in which Jesus fed the multitudes with nothing more than a few fish and some loaves of bread.

Mama loved the multitudes, the bigger the crowd the better as far as she was concerned. She never worried too much about having enough to feed everybody. Her way of working an everyday miracle was to "Put the big pot in the little pot!"

Literally, she meant that when you take a small amount of food out of a big container and put it into a little container, you automatically create the pleasing illusion of more food. Figuratively, she meant, "Make do." Everything will be alright, she was telling us when she clapped her hands and called out, "Put the big pot in the little pot!" She trusted that people would show up with extra provisions. She trusted her guests would take smaller portions to make sure everyone got their share. She always kept her door open. She always made room at our table for Mr. Albert and for anyone else who might need a hot meal.

She believed God would provide. She also believed God needed a little help and imagination from us.

Mama's kind of faith is the faith that has moved me forward. She taught me to have a confident faith and wield it to serve. As I grew older and began to recognize many inequities around me, I learned from other mentors, teachers, and heroes how to wield faith to fight injustice.

Just as the roots of the mulberry tree are extensive and deep in the earth, so the oppression of the weak and spiral of violence have always been the underbelly of human history; their roots are deep in our human psyche and our social institutions.

We do not need to settle for this. We don't have to accept patterns of oppression and violence that seem so rooted and ingrained in our culture. Our faith, however small, can uproot these old destructive patterns and replace them with caring and reconciled relationships—especially with the most marginalized in our world.

With God's grace present, hopefully we will become more a community formed in the image of Jesus. Our hearts alone will determine if this is happening. If our hearts are more grateful than when we began, we will know we are moving in the right direction.

When we do, we start to become more like Aunt Mollie and Aunt Kate, like Mr. Albert and Mama. When we do, we begin to understand the words: "We are worthless servants, we have done no more than our duty."

> Blessed are those who learn the way to serve, for they shall know the true meaning of worth.

PART III
Change Your World

Father Dan Richardson with Charles in front of the Assumption on the day of his first communion in 1951.

9

Father Dan

FROM THE TIME I WAS VERY YOUNG, I thought I might want to become a priest. The idea took hold of me because a father figure came into my life. Father Daniel S. Richardson became the pastor of the Assumption, just a stone's throw from where we lived at 1212 Seventh Avenue North, soon after Daddy died.

The previous pastor, the one who gave Daddy the last rites, was Father Aaron T. Gildea. He was stern and imposing; everyone called him by his last name with a little fear in their voices.

I was only about six years old, but I remember distinctly the day we learned, during Mass, that Father Gildea had accepted a new assignment, and another pastor was taking his place. I remember feeling such relief. I was just at the age when I was expected to become an acolyte, and I was terrified to serve Mass for Father Gildea because he was known to throw acolytes who made mistakes off the altar.

I don't remember thinking much about who the new pastor might be; I had no idea he was about to change the course of my life.

Nobody ever called our new pastor by his last name. We all called him Father Dan. He was dynamic, witty, and wise. And from the day he arrived at the Assumption, he made our parish church feel less like a place of worship and more like a welcoming home. Just like my own home down the street.

Mama, in particular, was a big fan of Father Dan. They were both funny and got a kick out of each other. Also, Mama needed a father figure for her children and saw in him somebody who could fill that role—somebody who had a gentle authority, like Daddy. "Be good or I'll tell Father Dan!" she would cry out whenever we fought, a threat she never followed through on.

Mama also loved to tell the story of when I was about seven and woke up one morning feeling awful. She was hurrying to get us off to school and catch the bus to work. I called out, "Mama, I don't feel good!" She came bustling in, put her hand on my hot forehead, and said, "Don't worry, you'll be okay. Aunt Mollie will take care of you."

But I didn't feel okay, I felt miserable. As she was trying to leave, I said, "Mama, I really don't feel good!" Exasperated, she blurted out, "Well, I guess you're gonna die!" as she headed out of the bedroom and made for the front door.

Before she could leave the house, I called out again, "Mama, call Father Dan!" She came back into the bedroom and said, "Why should I call Father Dan?"

"I need to go to confession."

"Why do you need to go to confession?"

"Because you said I'm gonna die. I need to go to confession and receive the last rites."

This broke her up. "Oh, you're not gonna die!" She called out, running over to hold me close. "But you're worrying me to death, and I've got to get to work!"

I can still hear her cackling as she finally made it out the door. On her way back home at the end of the workday, she stopped off at Assumption to tell Father Dan. He got as big a kick out of me thinking I was dying as she did. Neither one ever let me forget it.

As the years went on, I came to understand why we all loved Father Dan so much. It was because he loved and respected us so much. We were a poor parish, and we didn't get a lot of respect, but Father Dan made us believe we were special people living in a special part of town—worthy of the highest respect.

I came to realize Father Dan didn't just serve the poor. He loved the poor. He preferred the poor.

I wanted to be like him. I began to believe I had a vocation to do the same thing. At some point during high school, I decided to enter the seminary.

> Blessed are they who prefer living among the poor. Their choice changes lives.

Father Dan with Charles at his eighth-grade graduation in 1957.

10

Prof Al

I BEGAN MY POST-SECONDARY education at St. Mary's College in St. Mary's, Kentucky. At the time, it was the third largest Catholic college for young men in the nation, founded in 1821. This was where I had many formative experiences that solidified my decision to become a priest.

While at St. Mary's, I studied under the tutelage of a professor named Aloysius Lesousky, who taught English and Greek. We called him Prof Al.

One day during a break in class, Prof Al told us he was celebrating his fiftieth year teaching Greek. He was very proud of this accomplishment and said he was the only living professor in the United States who had taught Greek at a Catholic institution for half a century.

I remember saying, "Prof Al, not only are you the only living professor who has taught Greek for fifty years at a Catholic institution, you're probably the only person in the world who's taught Greek for fifty years at any institution."

This seemed to annoy him. He asked, "Mr. Strobel, can you prove that?" I said, "Prove it? No, it's just kind of obvious. Who else is there?" Prof Al responded gruffly, "If you can't prove it, don't say it."

In the course of his teaching, Prof Al asked our class, "Have you read the Sermon on the Mount?" Not everyone had. He said, "Go read it."

Prof Al told us that he read the Sermon on the Mount every day because of the teachings it contained, and he was proud to pass on its crucial words.

Charles as a student at St. Mary's College in Kentucky.

I thought, "If it means that much to Prof Al, I need to read it and try to learn it." Because of his influence, I have always had a special love for the Sermon on the Mount, which became the core of my value system.

After graduating from St. Mary's College, I moved to Washington, DC, to continue my studies at the Theological College of Catholic University of America. There, my love for the Sermon on the Mount deepened as I came to realize the importance of its core teaching that God loves the poor. I based every scripture project, term paper, and essay on it.

The part of it that has stayed with me most has been the Beatitudes.

The Beatitudes introduce the Sermon on the Mount. Matthew presents Jesus as the new Moses proclaiming these Beatitudes as blessings to his followers. Like Moses, who went up on the mountain to receive the Ten Commandments, Jesus went up on a hillside to deliver his Sermon on the Mount.

Because Jesus is presented as the new Moses, the Beatitudes are often explained as a new set of Laws—a new set of "dos" and "don'ts." But this can be deceiving, for Jesus seems to be concerned in other passages about creating a new moral compass that doesn't reside in the Law.

Jesus quotes the prophet Isaiah: "These people pay me lip service, but their hearts are far from me." And in another passage, he says, "It is not what goes into a man's mouth that makes him unclean; it is what comes out of his mouth; and what comes out of his mouth originates in the mind." In other words, Jesus says that life with God does not begin in the external observance of the Law, but it originates inside our hearts and minds. And he yearns for us to become aware of that inner life of the soul.

If the Beatitudes are not laws, what are they? I prefer scripture scholar Joachim Jeremias's explanation that they are not external norms for us to follow, for he says that laws can cause us to feel condemned and to feel as though we can never measure up. Laws force us to be compliant. They lead to shame and guilt, and the understanding of ourselves as sinful beings. Laws call us to perfection that we must live out—or call us to repentance because we have failed to live them out.

But, unlike the Ten Commandments, the Beatitudes are not laws. They are experiences of faith or examples of a living faith, blessings that lift our spirits. The phrase "blessed are you" frees us from feeling condemnation from the Law and allows us to experience life with God deep inside our soul. The Beatitudes are illustrations—examples—of the Gospel, the Good News.

The Beatitudes become the description of what a life of faith looks like.

And Beatitude Moments are experiences that affect all the other ordinary moments of our lives. The more we experience Beatitude Moments, the richer our lives will be. As examples, they are limitless in their expression. They are expressions of our faith lived out.

For example, almost every woman who has ever given birth to a child understands how bringing a child into the world will always be a blessing that sustains her and her child for the rest of her life. Regardless of all the trouble and difficult circumstances that come in raising that child from day to day, she will never forget the experience of childbirth. It will remain for her a blessed moment.

> Blessed is the mother in childbirth, for the bond she receives will never be broken.

11

The *Anawim*

AS I HAVE MENTIONED, I grew up among poor people who were good to one another, good to my family, and good to me. We all helped each other through hard times and celebrated together the good times. I cherished the memory of my father, a man of modest means who nonetheless considered himself rich in all the ways that truly mattered. I watched my mother stretch her small salary to the limit to make sure we had food, clothes and shelter, yet she was so happy and grateful for the life we had and the neighborhood we called home. I was drawn from a very early age to poor people and to those, like Father Dan, who exalted poor people.

But at Catholic University—where, from 1965 to 1969, I continued my studies for the priesthood and earned a master's degree in theology—I came to understand in the classroom that the poor of the world not only should be but *must be* at the top of the list of our concerns as a society.

Starting with the Hebrew and Christian scriptures, I heard over and over words like the prophet's call to "defend the widow, the orphan and the stranger"; or the psalmist proclaim, "the Lord hears the cries of the poor," or, "lavishly God gives to the poor," or "God lifts up the lowly to high places," or "go sell your possessions and give to the poor." And dozens and dozens and dozens of other passages.

But nothing struck me with such force as when my scripture professor unfolded the meaning of a beautiful word in Hebrew, little known and rarely used—a word that gave fullness and depth to everything I intuitively believed and understood about the so-called "least of these." The word is *anawim*. *Anawim* is the Hebrew word for "poor." But it is so much more.

Rather than describing an economic condition, the word refers to all of us, as we are seen by God. Jesus proclaims in the first Beatitude, "Blessed are the poor." This is a bad translation for "Blessed are *the anawim*."

Anawim defines all of us—every man, woman and child—as a blessing. Our blessing is that we know we are incapable of being happy all by ourselves. This is our poverty, and all the riches in the world cannot rid us of it.

If we need to, we can prove it to ourselves. For as soon as we become honest and aware of what it means to live and breathe and embrace the gift of a new day dawning that comes as a total gift, not as our entitlement, we have to come to grips with poverty—not as something to avoid, but as something essential to living a life of love. Spiritual writings over the centuries say there is no possible conversion unless one experiences a poverty of self. This is at the heart of the meaning of *anawim*.

The *anawim* are not simply the ones without change in their pockets. The *anawim* are all of us as seen by God. Yet most of us resist thinking of ourselves as poor, much less blessed in our poverty. We lose sight of the fact that this is how we are created. At our birth, long before we achieve power, prestige, possessions, or even pigmentation, we are naked, vulnerable, and poor.

When we forget this basic truth about ourselves—whether we are people of faith or not—we end up fighting for our own survival rather than helping each other survive.

As we gather possessions, power, and prestige, we begin to separate, creating all kinds of differences of class and status. Although almost everyone believes in the necessity of possessions, the differences they create inspire extreme competition, rivalry, and war. From the cultural existence of nations, states, tribes, clans, castes, and social classes to the more informal groupings in congregations, clubs, associations, businesses, and teams, our separation can diminish our realization of this divine truth proclaimed from the beginning: We share a common humanity. We share a common poverty.

But understanding ourselves as the *anawim* establishes an equality among us that can lead to the greatest blessing imaginable—human kindness. Rather than allowing our riches to divide us, we can discipline ourselves to recognize how each of us is the same. We can be united in a poverty that yields a generosity of spirit.

> Blessed are the poor. Blessed are the *anawim*. Blessed are all of us. Amen.

12

Ol' Grange

THE CHAPTERS IN THIS PART of my story are about leaving the warm cocoon of my childhood and becoming an adult. My favorite sport was central to my transition from boy to man, from innocence to experience.

The evening I drove home in Horace Tidwell's car and began my long relationship with baseball on the radio, I also became a faithful listener and fan of Larry Munson, the Nashville Vol's incomparable announcer. Night after night after night, I was glued to our old Motorola as Munson wove the tale of the Vols' odyssey through a 154-game season.

Munson was a master storyteller. There were other famous announcers like Mel Ott, Red Barber, and Dizzy Dean, but no one matched Munson in my estimation. His cadence, phrasing, tone, and descriptive details added all the elements of excitement, anticipation, conflict, disappointment, and success appropriately ascribed to real drama. He gave the game a heart and a soul and then made me feel its pulse:

> Down in the bullpen, warming up again, is ol' Pistol Pete Modica. Gosh, you've gotta wonder, how many times can Poland go to him? Yet it looks like Poland's gonna make a change. He could bring in the lefty, Cal Howe, but we'll see.
>
> And here he comes making that long walk from down in the bullpen in left, and he's dragging his right arm behind him. How long can this guy keep pitchin'? It seems like every night he has to be up throwin'. So here we go again.

He's on the mound now bringing along with him all his 150 pounds of flesh. He's starting his slow windup now and slinging that wiry arm out there like a whip.

Munson had me and hundreds of others riveted to the action, whether it was the slow part of the game, like the changing of a pitcher, or the fast pace of a so-called "bam-bam-bam" 6 to 4 to 3 double-play.

With each turn of events, he drew from me all kinds of reactions. I was carried along, over the course of two or three hours, on an unpredictable emotional ride. Inning after inning, batter after batter, pitch after pitch. I kept detailed score in my notebook as I listened along. There was the groan after a strikeout with the bases loaded, the pride over a perfectly executed double play, the disappointment at an error, the thrill of a game-winning home run, the nail-biting during a crucial pitcher's jam, the sudden surprise when a runner was picked off, the anger at an umpire's bad call, the staccato clapping to ignite a rally, and the urgent plea for a clutch hit.

And of course, there was the constant buzz of the crowd, rising and falling in the background with the action. The crowd noise lifted me from my spot on the sofa and delivered me right into the stands, moaning and groaning and cheering along with my fellow fans.

It was that very crowd noise that, one night during my first season listening to the Vols, drew me into a mystery that would continue for the rest of my boyhood.

At some point between innings, during a lull in the game, I heard a lone voice call out. It was fuzzy, but it sounded like a man saying, "C'mon Ol' Grange! Hit a couple a home runs!"

What was that? Who said that? What's that guy talking about? Was there a player on the other team named Grange? I knew there wasn't a Vols player with that name because I knew every Vols player by heart.

A few innings later, I heard the voice again.

"C'mon Ol' Grange! Hit a couple a home runs!"

This time I checked the roster. No opposing player named Grange. I double-checked the Vols roster. Maybe they'd called someone up from Double A. Nope. No Grange.

The next night, another game by the radio. And I heard the guy again.

"C'mon Ol' Grange! Hit a couple a home runs!"

Now I was really bothered. Who was this voice? And who was Ol' Grange? I had to find out.

I called Jerry—our Daddy had nicknamed him "Butch"—into the living room. "Butch, come here! Listen!" I said.

We hovered over the radio.

I asked, "Did you hear it?"

"Hear what?" he said.

"That voice! It sounds like he's saying, 'Come on Ol' Grange! Hit a couple a home runs!' I hear this voice every game. I'm trying to figure out who it is. Maybe he's an usher at the stadium? But he even seems to be at the away games. Last night we were in Birmingham and tonight we're in Mobile. And still the same voice. Could he be a sportswriter who travels with the Vols? Or a fan who goes to every game? Listen!"

Jerry leaned in. His eyes widened as he heard the voice too: "Come on Ol' Grange! Hit a couple a home runs!"

"Did you hear it, Butch?"

"Yes! But why is he saying that?" Jerry asked.

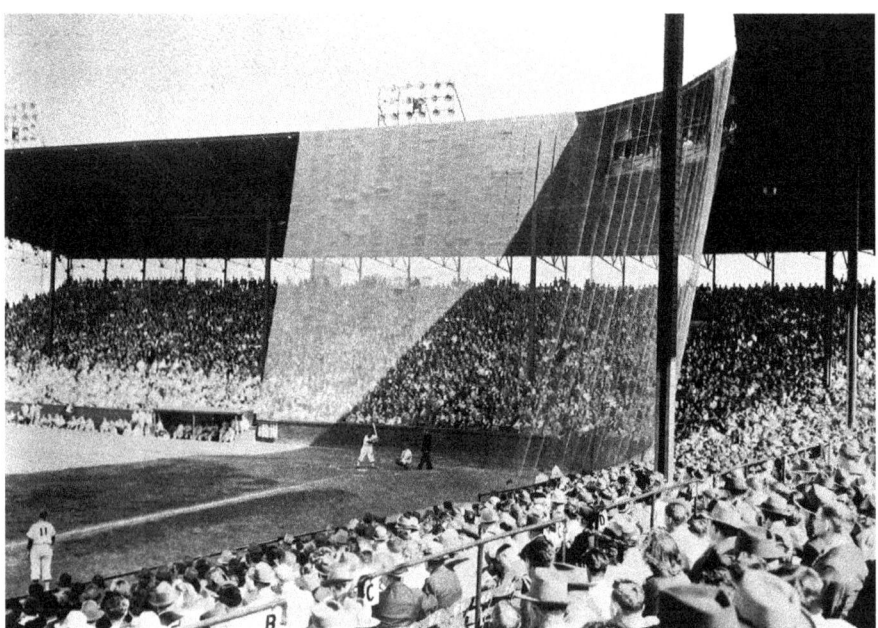

Sulphur Dell baseball field in North Nashville.

He had a point. It wasn't a phrase you hear in baseball. It didn't make sense. Nobody says, "Hit a couple a home runs." You hit a home run or not, but you don't hit two at the same time. We listened again and again, game after game. Could the voice be talking about Red Grange? But he was a famous football player, not a baseball player. We had many ideas, but none of them seemed to make sense.

So went my nights—spring through fall—ear fixed to the Vols games on the radio. Unless, of course, I was lucky enough to be there in person. When the Nashville Vols played at home, I always tried to make the three-block sprint to Sulfur Dell to watch. I knew the ushers. They opened the gates after the seventh inning, letting those of us without tickets in. I watched as long as I could, aware of my curfew at 11 p.m. Just before the clock hit eleven, I raced home.

On the way, I ran along Jefferson Street past a corner restaurant run by Good Jelly Jones. Some ladies who worked in the apartments upstairs would be sitting in the windows. They would see me coming and yell, "C'mon little boy! Come up here and let us tell you some stories!" Then they laughed uproariously. I waved and laughed. I wasn't afraid. But I kept on running.

Dashing into the house, right to that radio dial, I begged Mama to let me hear the end of the game even though I had promised her I would finish my homework. And season after season, I listened for Ol' Grange.

Only as I became a teenager did I begin to accept that the anonymous voice—and Ol' Grange—was going to remain one of life's many mysteries. I finally put him to rest and again turned my focus fully to Munson's play-by-play. He was my teacher, and I was a student of the game that mirrored, for me, what life was meant to be about.

> Blessed are those who learn to live in mystery. They shall find delight.

❋ 13 ❋

Larry Munson

IN THE MID-1950S, the city of Nashville began to change, as did its relationship with baseball. The Vols were part of the Southern Association of minor league teams. After Jackie Robinson broke baseball's color barrier in 1946, the Southern Association refused to integrate. More and more, this turned fans away from the Vols. A local group of businessmen tried to resurrect the team in 1959, selling $25 shares to local investors. But in 1961, when the Southern Association collapsed for lack of fan interest, so did the team.

A last gasp to field another Nashville team in the Double-A Atlantic League sputtered out in 1963 when it finished in last place. So ended baseball in Nashville for the next fourteen years. Sulphur Dell—that shining beacon in North Nashville along the Cumberland River—was converted into a racetrack in 1965. Then it was turned into a tow lot before finally meeting the wrecking ball in 1969.

In my own way, I too was moving on by the mid-1960s, immersing myself in my studies and in the Civil Rights movement in Washington, DC. As an impressionable, eager young man far from North Nashville, my entire world seemed to be expanding. Even baseball was going through a metamorphosis. Up until the 1950s, only ten cities had teams. Some had two. But then things started to shift. The Saint Louis Browns went East to Baltimore and became the Orioles. The Kansas City Athletics headed out to Oakland. In 1966, the South secured its first Major League Team when the Milwaukee Braves moved to Atlanta.

Larry Munson during his years as the voice of the Georgia Bulldogs.

And the person chosen as the color analyst for the Braves, the man who would lead the South through play-by-plays of its first major league games, was the announcer of my youth—my guide to every Vols game—the legendary Larry Munson.

Home from DC that February of 1966, I sat down with a copy of the Sunday *Tennessean* to read all about Munson's move. The title of the story, by reporter Kathy Sawyer, captured everything I felt about Munson: "Almost Like Being There: That's What His Fans Say about a Munson Sportscast."

Munson reminisced about the old days when he covered the Vols. He explained how he would announce the away games by reading off the Western Union wire, adding noises in the background along the way to make it seem real.

"The technique takes imagination and a bit of acting," Munson said. "The broadcaster reads the play-by-play off the wire as it is transmitted, as though he were actually at the game, with sound effects of different types of crowd noises in the background."

I dropped the paper into my lap.

I read the phrase, "with sound effects of different types of crowd noises in the background" again and again, howling with laughter.

The mystery of my youth was solved.

I shouted to Jerry, "Butch! Butch! Ol' Grange didn't exist! He was just a tape recording! Munson made him up! He was just a tape!"

I had spent years wondering. Now I knew. The voice in the crowd and Ol' Grange—they were only alive in the mind of a boy.

Was I a fool for believing they were real? Never. That was the magic of Munson. That was the magic of childhood. And that is the magic of baseball.

My hero provided color commentary for the Braves for just a few months before becoming the play-by-play announcer for the University of Georgia Bulldogs. He made the position his own for more than four decades and became a legend among Georgia football fans. He retired in 2008 and died in 2011.

> Blessed are they who wield their creativity for others. The magic they make never fades away.

EDITORS' NOTE: *Minor league baseball returned to Nashville in 1978, when Greer Stadium at Fort Negley opened as the home of the Nashville Sounds. Charlie became a devoted Sounds fan, and often went to games with friends or by himself. He told his niece Katie the story of the day he attended a game by himself at Greer and caught his first foul ball:*

In all the years I'd been going to games since I was young—minor league, major league, college—I'd never caught a hit or a foul. I'd always been hopeful, but it never happened.

Then one day at a Sounds game, a foul ball came right at me, like it was meant for me. I caught it with my bare hands. I couldn't believe it! I was looking at the ball, rolling it around in my hands, savoring the moment, when I noticed a little kid was standing beside me, just staring at me. He didn't say a word, just kept staring.

I thought, "No! I am not giving this kid this ball! I've waited my whole life to catch this ball! I'll give him anything else, the shirt off my back, all the money in my wallet, but not this ball."

He just stood there, staring. He wouldn't leave! I tried to ignore him. But he kept tormenting me until I couldn't take it anymore. "Fine," I finally said, "Take it." He smiled and grabbed it and took off. And I've never caught another one!

14

Dr. Martin Luther King Jr.

APRIL 4, 1968, STARTED AS AN ORDINARY DAY in my life. It was the Thursday before Palm Sunday, and my thoughts were full of preparations to leave Catholic University for a week-long spring break. I had finished my examinations. I was making plans to drive home to Nashville in my pale green, rusty 1963 Chevy II Nova with a group of fellow seminarians from Tennessee. My cousin Carl Strobel had given me the car when I left for Catholic U. He wouldn't take a dime for it.

As the day progressed, I remember hearing about the Civil Rights march in support of the striking sanitation workers in Memphis. The big news was that Dr. Martin Luther King Jr. would lead the march. Dr. King's presence galvanized attention on the march and the strike that precipitated it. While law enforcement officials reassured Memphians that protests would be peaceful, the atmosphere was tense.

I was aware of the march, although not paying too much attention to the specifics. The main thing on my mind was getting out of Washington and enjoying a full week of vacation from school and responsibilities.

We had a large TV room in our house of studies where all the students would gather to watch the news, sports, and cultural events. As the dinner hour approached, more and more seminarians began to fill up the space to its capacity of 150. The conversation became more serious as several students began talking about going to Memphis to support the striking workers.

I found the idea fascinating. But I was undecided about going.

Then, around 7 p.m., Walter Cronkite broke into the CBS evening news with the shocking announcement that Dr. King had been shot and killed at the Lorraine Motel in Memphis. We all looked at one another in disbelief and horror.

The death of President John Kennedy five years earlier in November 1963 was still fresh in our nation's mind. His assassination united the country in grief and sorrow. But those of us who were young and idealistic also believed a new age was being born.

Lyndon Johnson's succeeding presidency in 1964 brought the War on Poverty as a keystone of his Great Society. A new generation, to which I belonged, was hoping to take the lead in ushering in such a world.

But then came the Vietnam War, sucking us into a deep quagmire that seemed to get deeper every day. Those of us who were students saw the insanity of such a war and screamed out for peace.

Dr. King was among those we looked to for leadership, both on equal rights and against the war. In April 1967, exactly a year before he was assassinated, Dr. King said:

> This confused war has played havoc with our domestic destinies. Despite feeble protestations to the contrary, the promises of The Great Society have been shot down on the battlefields of Vietnam. The pursuit of this widened war has narrowed the promised dimensions of the domestic welfare programs, making the poor—white and Negro—bear the heaviest burdens, both at the front and at home.

As one who grew up among the poor, and as one who was learning in the classroom that the poor should be first among society's priorities, I was moved and inspired by everything Dr. King preached. I believed he could lead us out of the wilderness of violence and bigotry.

Now he was dead, slaughtered by hate. I was devastated.

I remember what happened immediately after we heard the news of his death. Our only pay telephone started ringing, and quickly the word spread of a memorial service at St. Stephen's and the Incarnation Episcopal Church, which was across town from Catholic U. Everyone rushed to jump in their cars to get there. Five or six of us crammed into my Chevy II and we took off.

Traffic was horrible and we could sense the anger on the streets. We were watchful; we understood the potential for violence. What we didn't anticipate was the outrage.

As we drove, we crossed Fourteenth Street. News of the assassination was only an hour old, but Fourteenth Street was already in flames and people were rioting. Suddenly, we were right in the middle of it. We could see flames up and down the street for blocks. People were hurling rocks and bottles, overturning trash cans, setting cars on fire or overturning them while yelling, "Revolution!," "Kill the honkies!," and "Bastards!"

We had to drive through debris, trash, and flames, trying to avoid flat tires, gunshots, firehoses, burst water pipes, broken glass, and ruptured fire hydrants. I remember thinking we would never make it. I remember people around us screaming, "Don't stop! If you stop, you're dead!"

Somehow, we arrived at St. Stephen's for the service. Everyone had rushed to get there, but the gravity of the situation was so great that no one knew what to say or do once we were assembled. I remember some feeble attempts to express appropriate words, presumably consoling or inspiring. I remember a few hymns, but they were not a balm to ease our devastation.

Later we drove around and around aimlessly, observing all the other aimlessness we saw. We noticed the growing presence of the police, soldiers, and the National Guard, who were positioned on every street corner, creating security checkpoints. As the inferno on Fourteenth Street spread to other streets, more and more fires lit the darkness. Gunshots and sirens became the noise of the night.

When we got back to Catholic U.'s Theological College later that evening, we stayed up the rest of the night fixed on the television screen, which played over and over scenes of Dr. King's last hours, of the Lorraine Motel balcony, and of his "I've been to the mountaintop" speech. We were riveted by his final words:

> Well, I don't know what will happen now. We've got some difficult days ahead. But it really doesn't matter with me now, because I've been to the mountaintop. And I don't mind. Like anybody, I would like to live a long life. Longevity has its place. But I'm not concerned about that now. I just want to do God's will. And He's allowed me to go up to the mountain. And I've looked over. And

I've seen the Promised Land. I may not get there with you. But I want you to know tonight, that we, as a people, will get to the Promised Land! And so I'm happy, tonight. I'm not worried about anything. I'm not fearing any man! Mine eyes have seen the glory of the coming of the Lord!

Again and again and again we listened. And then we sat around and talked and talked about what to do next—about what was next for each of us in the immediate days ahead and about what was next for our world.

After going off to bed for a few hours, we greeted the dawn. Many of us climbed to the roof of our five-story building to look out over the city. We saw an eerie scene. All across the horizon, clouds of smoke were rising from different pockets of DC.

Everyone has seen dark, black smoke against the sky suggesting a huge fire in the distance. But what we saw that morning was more like a scene from a European city during World War II after a night of bombing. Dozens of swirls of smoke were rising in all directions, and right in the middle of that horizon, enveloped by those black clouds, were the Capitol and the Washington Monument.

We came down from the roof sullen and sad. The rector had announced that the college would be closing, and all the students needed to leave Washington. There was fear of race riots in the city, and our safety demanded that we get out of town. We were faced with mundane details: calling home, packing, and arranging transportation.

I remember calling Mama and asking how everyone was. Living in North Nashville might be risky now, I thought, for we were in an integrated neighborhood adjacent to Nashville's African American community, which was centered around Jefferson Street.

I knew we had good relations with all our neighbors; still, the African American community had suffered the most monumental blow of my lifetime and was rightly enraged by Dr. King's assassination. Who knew what might happen? Mama told me things were calm and encouraged me to "just pray."

Within a few hours, all of us from Nashville—Pat Thompson, George Frazier, Mike Weber, and I—had piled into the car of another seminarian, who was able to drive us out of DC to Chattanooga, where we bought Greyhound bus tickets home.

It was a long trip. Leaving on Friday afternoon, we traveled all night. My first memory, as we arrived in Nashville around 9 a.m. Saturday morning, was driving up Fifth Avenue North and looking out the window and seeing the Downtown Presbyterian Church. Then I noticed the streets and how empty they were. There were only a few cars and practically no pedestrians. I remember thinking, "This is like a deserted town, a ghost town."

Easter fell on April 14 that year. Between the day we rolled into town on that Greyhound and the day we rolled back out again a few days after Easter, I stayed at home or close to it. My family and I were in full attendance for Holy Week services down the street at the Assumption. But Dr. King's death was a pall over everything.

I remember how real Good Friday seemed that week, compared to other years. Most of all, I remember thinking how much more difficult it was to believe the Easter story. Or how easily I found myself in the sorrows of those early disciples who seemed so desolate for having lost someone they loved, someone who didn't deserve to die, someone whom they counted on to lead them.

I couldn't imagine feeling any lower. But there was more to come. Two months later, on June 5, Senator Robert F. Kennedy was assassinated at the Ambassador Hotel in Los Angeles while celebrating his Democratic Party primary wins in California and South Dakota. Kennedy was another champion of the poor. His death compounded the social unrest roiling the nation.

By then, the Civil Rights Movement was in full swing, and I was fully immersed in it. I took every opportunity I could to participate, most memorably by visiting Resurrection City, the makeshift community of more than three thousand poor people from all over the country that was established on the National Mall just a few weeks after Dr. King's murder. Led by Dr. Ralph Abernathy, the goal was to build an encampment of the nation's most needy right in the shadow of the Lincoln Memorial, visually drawing attention to their numbers and their plight as their leaders lobbied Congress for better housing, education, health care, and wages.

I remember going there by myself, just to look around and take in the landscape. I recall being cautious at first, but then immediately wanting to be in solidarity with the residents of Resurrection City. I walked with them and talked with them. I recognized their concerns as the same concerns of the people who raised me.

I also was saddened that they did not get what they came for—that they would not be successful in their quest for better housing, health care, education, and wages. Resurrection City lasted for 42 days, just a little longer than Jesus spent in the desert. The government allowed the residents to protest, and then told them, seemingly on behalf of the nation, "Go away. We don't want to see you anymore. You're dirtying up the mall."

But I also learned from this experience and others that the response to failing is to keep trying. Don't give up.

The day of President Richard Nixon's inauguration on January 20, 1969, was a dark day for me. I viewed it as a backlash against the causes of Civil Rights and peace. I was down and dispirited. Many others among the seminarians and lay students at Catholic U. felt the same. They made plans to get together on inauguration day and mourn collectively.

But I made another plan. On January 20, 1969, I stayed by myself in my room the whole day in total darkness. I don't mean to suggest I curled up in bed and slept. I mean I drew the shades tightly and I stretched an army blanket around the crevices in my door so that absolutely no light could get into the room. It was my way of not giving the event any light whatsoever.

The next day, my friends were cracking up at my idiosyncratic form of protest—and so was I! But I taught myself something the day Nixon became president. Our response to injustice—even when we can do nothing—is to try to do something. Even if it's a protest of one.

Father Charles gives communion to his mother Mary Catherine and niece Katie Seigenthaler during his first Mass at the Assumption, February 1, 1970.

I was ordained a priest on January 31, 1970, at the Cathedral of the Incarnation in my hometown of Nashville. On my ordination memorial card, I chose to print a quote from Robert Kennedy, which read:

> Few of us will have the greatness to bend history itself, but each of us can work to change a small portion of events, and in the total of all those acts will be written the history of this generation. Each time a man stands up for an ideal or acts to improve the lot of others or strikes out against injustice, he sends

forth a tiny ripple of hope and crossing each other from a million different centers of energy and daring, those ripples build a current that can sweep down the mightiest walls of oppression and resistance.

> EDITORS' NOTE: *Pat Thompson was a lifelong friend of Charlie's. They were classmates at Father Ryan during the school year; counselors at Camp Marymount, Nashville's Catholic overnight camp, during the summer; and seminarians together at Catholic University. Pat remembers Charlie as a young man who relentlessly pursued what he believed in. He tells this story:*
>
> All of us from Nashville who were in the seminary at that time were committed to Civil Rights and took a special interest in the fact that one of the recipients of Dr. King's 1963 "Letter from a Birmingham Jail" was Nashville's Bishop Joseph Durick.* After he was named in the letter, Bishop Durick became very pro-integration, totally supportive of the Civil Rights Movement.
>
> Bishop Durick and Charlie became of the same mind on many things, although Charlie did have a couple of run-ins with him, mostly over his long hair! The principal at Knoxville Catholic High School, where Charlie taught for several years, wanted Charlie to cut his hair and was on Bishop Durick's case about it. So Bishop Durick was on Charlie's case. Well, Charlie wouldn't cut it. The more they tried to force him, the more he dug in.
>
> His point was why are you worried more about my hair than about poverty or racism? Of course, he was right. Charlie finally cut his hair when they stopped telling him to do it.
>
> * Dr. King's famous letter defending nonviolent resistance to segregation was addressed to eight moderate White religious leaders, Bishop Durick among them, who had denounced the demonstrations King was leading.

> Blessed are those who try to do something even when they can't do anything. They shall keep marching on.

15

Myles Horton

SOMETIME IN THE 1960S, I was driving my Chevy II on the Cumberland Plateau just east of Nashville near the small town of Monteagle, Tennessee. Suddenly, I saw a huge billboard up on Monteagle Mountain with a picture of Dr. King on it. Underneath the picture was a caption that read: "Martin Luther King, Jr. A Communist trained at the Highlander Folk School."

"What is the Highlander Folk School?" I wondered, and I thought, "If it had anything to do with training Dr. King, I want to know more about it."

Sometime later, I would learn that the Highlander Folk School trained not only Dr. King, but many other leaders of the Civil Rights movement in passive resistance and civil disobedience. Highlander had nothing to do with Communism as a political framework and everything to do with empowering poor and disenfranchised people to realize a more democratic and humane society that is inherently fair to everyone. Myles Horton co-founded Highlander in Monteagle in 1932 and was its most prominent leader.

Horton was born in 1905 in the small West Tennessee town of Savannah. His family was poor, but his parents taught school and were well-respected in the community because they helped others. The Hortons never thought of themselves or their neighbors as less than. In these ways, Horton's family reminded me of my own.

Horton believed in the power of education. He modeled Highlander after the Danish "folk schools," where adults learned how to harness collective action to change society for the good of all. Horton hoped to teach poor people in the United States strategies for organizing and taking control of their own lives and communities.

Highlander was integral to the labor movement of the 1930s in Appalachia and the southern United States. During the 1950s, it was critical to the success of the American Civil Rights Movement, training leaders such as Dr. King, Bernard Lafayette, Ralph Abernathy, John Lewis, and Rosa Parks. Because of the backlash it received (the billboard I saw encapsulated that backlash), the State of Tennessee revoked its charter and shut it down in 1961.

But Myles Horton refused to give up on the ideals of Highlander. He simply changed its name to the Highlander Research and Education Center and relocated it to Knoxville to continue its social justice work. In other words, he kept Highlander in the game.

Shortly after Horton died in 1990, I had the opportunity to speak with Laura McCray, an African American woman who was a champion of the poor in Nashville. She worked within her church community, Edgehill United Methodist Church, to found Luke 14:12, a program to feed and care for the poor. Known as "Miss Laura," she had also been active in the Civil Rights Movement and taken courses at Highlander with Rosa Parks, who became her good friend. She told me she was there the day Parks asked Myles Horton what she should do with the education she was receiving at Highlander. "Rosa," Horton said, "Go back and change your world."

I was extremely moved by Laura McCray's story and found myself retelling it on many occasions. Often, when I addressed audiences or talked to people one-on-one who wanted to know how they could make a difference, I would recount to them what Laura had heard Myles Horton say to Rosa Parks: "Go back and change your world."

As for Highlander, it lives on. Now located in New Market, Tennessee, it focuses on training leaders to advocate for environmental and related justice issues.

> Blessed are those who devote their lives to lifting up the poor. Their legacies will live forever.

As a newly ordained priest in the early 1970s, I took inspiration from Horton and others who insisted on marching forward on behalf of and in solidarity with the poor even in the face of headwinds.

I decided I wasn't going to let the 1960s be an idealized time in history for me, frozen in amber. I was going to try to carry it forward in my own life. I was going to keep playing, keep stepping up to the plate, keep showing up wherever I felt I was needed and could do the most good.

Immediately after my ordination, I taught theology for three years at Knoxville Catholic High School while living at the rectory of Immaculate Conception Church. I liked teaching but did not feel it was my calling. In my memory, it was during this time, around 1972, that I decided to make a pilgrimage to Highlander to visit Myles Horton. I felt called to serve the urban poor, like the people I'd grown up with and the people at Resurrection City. I needed inspiration and wanted the privilege of meeting an important, though mostly unknown, historical figure. I wanted to meet the man who had put theory into practice on behalf of the least of these.

I found Horton to be open to dialogue about Civil Rights and racial justice. He appreciated the fact that I was willing to listen to his story. I asked him about his life. He told me his family was poor but did not see poverty as shameful, which was my experience too. He reinforced my resolve to keep seeking justice for those whom society pushes to the margins.

After my third year at Knoxville Catholic, I asked my bishop for permission to live independently from the Immaculate Conception Church rectory.

Charlie in the early 1970s sporting the long hair he refused to cut.

I wanted to live in the community, where I felt I could be closer to the people I wanted to help.

This was a national trend at the time, but I was the first priest in my diocese to make the request. The bishop was not in favor, so I decided to take a leave of absence from the active priesthood. I worked as a counselor and taught a course at the University of Tennessee called Introduction to Human Services. I also opened an office of the National Conference of Christians and Jews in Knoxville.

> EDITORS' NOTE: *Msgr. Owen Campion and Charles both immersed themselves in the study of Jewish history and the persecution of the Jews over the centuries. They felt a responsibility for the role of the Catholic Church in Jewish persecution and conducted outreach to Jewish leaders and communities at every opportunity. Msgr. Campion tells this story:*
>
> ---
>
> Charles not only started the Knoxville Chapter of the National Conference of Christians and Jews, but he was very involved in the Nashville Chapter, which held an annual banquet. I remember one year, the organizers invited Father Edward Flannery to speak at the banquet; he was head of the Office of Jewish-Catholic Relations for the United States Conference of Catholic Bishops and the author of "The Anguish of the Jews," a study of antisemitism.
>
> Charles arranged to meet with Father Flannery beforehand, and they spent some time together. Several weeks later, I ran into Father Flannery in Washington, DC, and he said to me, "Your friend from Nashville, Charlie Strobel, really is an authority on antisemitism."
>
> That was Charles. He dove deeply into everything he cared about.

This was a productive time for me, but I still wasn't working on behalf of the poor in the way that I wanted. In 1975, the newly appointed bishop of Nashville, Bishop James Niedergeses, called to ask me to return to active ministry and take an assignment in the diocese. I asked to be assigned to an urban parish. He assured me he would do so as soon as an opening arose but, in the interim, he wanted to assign me to the position of associate pastor of Holy Rosary Parish in

Donelson, Tennessee. I spent a wonderful year there as the associate to Father William Bevington, Holy Rosary's pastor.

Bishop Niedergeses was as good as his word. In 1977, he gave me the assignment I had hoped for: pastor of Holy Name Catholic Church, located in a working-class urban neighborhood in East Nashville just across the Cumberland River from the city's downtown.

My years at Holy Name from 1977 to 1987 would be among the most consequential of my life.

Father Strobel receives a marquee welcome in 1975 to his first assignment in the Nashville diocese: assistant pastor of Holy Rosary Catholic Church in Donelson, Tennessee.

PART IV

Room In The Inn

16

Mrs. Hopwood

I LOVED HOLY NAME FROM THE START but was initially overwhelmed by the responsibility I had been given.

Many of the parishioners didn't have much to call their own and they kept coming to the rectory for multiple needs, such as clothing and food. We kept a lot of donated clothes on hand to give away, but I had no idea how to cook. I did know how to make a peanut butter and jelly sandwich and had been handing them out from the front door of Twelve-Twelve since I was big enough to open it. So I began slapping them together for hungry people who came by Holy Name. Soon enough, I found myself making them all the time.

I remember commenting to Mary Hopwood, who worked for Holy Name, "I don't know what else we do around here. All I seem to do is hand out peanut butter and jelly sandwiches!"

She just laughed and smiled, never contradicting me but also never seeming as flustered as I was.

Mary Magdalene Hopwood—or "Itty" as everyone called her—was one of those people who could wear many different hats at the same time and with ease: housekeeper, secretary, cook, bookkeeper, receptionist, sacristan, and any other job, large or small, required of her.

Mary Hopwood was remarkable for many reasons, such as being the mother of twelve children prior to starting her

Mary Hopwood

second "career" at Holy Name. She was hired at age fifty-five and served in the role for more than twenty-five years, ten of those years while I was pastor. In every sense of the word, she was co-pastor of the parish. Often—both in teasing and in seriousness—I told her and others that she was, in fact, the pastor in so many ways. Everything I did, she could do as well, if not better.

She impressed me like no other person I've ever known because of the way she lived her life. For the ten years I was at Holy Name, I witnessed her work ten to twelve hours a day. During that time, there were many opportunities for her to make missteps, simply because there were thousands of situations that came our way—knocks at the door, rings of the telephone, and all the other day-to-day happenings of a church office. But she never once uttered a frustrated or unkind word. She never once uttered a spiteful, angry, cynical, disappointed, or discouraging one. She was a woman who always offered words of kindness and love—and even more remarkable actions. In a highly sensitive workplace, she kept every confidence. Every secret was safe with her. Everyone who met her over the telephone or in person came away with a wonderful sense of her loving presence.

A local homeless man named Doy terrorized the parish with his demands. We replaced the storm door at the rectory several times after he kicked it in. His language was X-rated, and he stayed on the porch all day long demanding his just due. I was the object of a lot of his venom. I would pay him off just to get him to go away, like extortion. Mama would say, "Doy is your ticket to heaven." I'd reply, "If he's my ticket, I don't want to go."

Everyone in the parish wanted to avoid him and—even worse—was afraid of him. Everyone, except Mary Hopwood. She always spoke quietly and respectfully to Doy. She was the only one who would listen to him, even though his mental state was irrational and rambling, and she was the only one he would listen to.

In time, I realized that I didn't really love Doy as Mrs. Hopwood did. I only wanted to change him. I was disrespecting him and so I got disrespect in return. Once I realized that he was not my problem to solve but my brother to love, the change was almost immediate. I changed and he changed, and we grew to know and love each other. Doy became my master, and I became his servant. I was with him when he died.

> Blessed are those who teach us to love everyone,
> for they are the best teachers of all.

17

Lulabelle

EDITORS' NOTE: *Not everyone who had a major impact on Charles Strobel's life was a human being. During much of the time Charlie was pastor of Holy Name, his constant companion was Lulabelle, a black-and-white cocker spaniel mix.*

Msgr. Campion also had a special relationship with Lulabelle, whom they both called "Lu." He tells the story:

Lu was a gift. She was a shelter dog. Charles was not her first owner and the previous owner had been very abusive. Well, Charles was determined to relieve her of the trauma she had experienced and draw her out. He always kept her very close and was very gentle with her.

Of course, she came to trust him and Mrs. Hopwood right away, but it took her quite a while to be convinced that all the other people who came and went from the rectory weren't going to hit her. Though she was never hostile, early on she would get frantic and hide.

But over time, Lu and I also developed a bond. Soon enough, she was involved in every conversation Charles and I had—and we realized she was quite the philosopher!

We came to rely heavily on her advice.

Charles would call me and say collections at Holy Name were down, and then he'd say, "But I talked it over with Lu and she said, 'That's another thing

Charles with his niece Katie Eadler, Father Owen Campion, and their favorite philosopher, Lulabelle.

you all came up with—money. When we need anything, we just take it and if we don't need it, we leave it for somebody else!'"

One day I heard Charles had hurt his back playing baseball or some sport. I called him and said, "I was discussing this with Lu, and she said, 'He walks funny on two legs anyway. Tell him to get down on all fours and he'll feel better.'"

Then Charles would call me to say the electricity had gone out, but Lu had told him, "That's another thing you all came up with—electricity. Just go to bed. Night's a time to sleep, not worry about lights."

The whole tone of our Lulabelle discourse was, "You humans are so damn dumb and have made a huge mess of everything and you need to start listening to dogs." She set us straight on so many occasions.

Lu lived to be at least twelve years old and started to fail around the time Mrs. Hopwood did. I remember the day Charles knew he was going to have to put her to sleep. Before he took her to the vet, he took her over to say goodbye to Mrs. Hopwood.

We buried Lu in the backyard at Veronica's house.* Veronica was quite the animal lover and had an impressive pet cemetery. Lu drew a crowd that day; she was beloved. Charles was digging the grave when I arrived. As he was laying her into it, he said, "Well Lu, not many dogs have a funeral this big!"

Not long after, he either got a cat or started feeding one that came to the rectory door, I can't remember which. He told me about it, and I said, "Lu told me before she died that she wouldn't be gone six weeks before you'd take up with a cat."

* Veronica Strobel-Seigenthaler was Charles's sister and eldest sibling. She died in 2022.

18

Michael "Bear" Hodges

BY THE WINTER OF 1985, I had been the pastor of Holy Name for eight years and was hoping for many more. In 1983, my propensity to pass out peanut butter and jelly sandwiches had morphed into Holy Name's Loaves and Fishes Community Meal. I was also working with houses of worship of all denominations throughout East Nashville, an outgrowth of my interest in ecumenism, to take care of the most destitute among our congregations.

But one night changed everything. As I looked out my second-story bedroom window in the rectory, which was beside the church, I saw a disturbing scene. A number of cars were parked in the church parking lot, and I could tell people were bedding down in them even as the temperature was dropping below freezing.

I was compelled to do something. I went down and invited everyone inside to spend the night in our church cafeteria.

I didn't think too long about it, probably because I knew I would talk myself out of it. As the pastor, I knew the consequences of such a decision were far greater than simply giving a dozen men one night's lodging. What would I do the next night when they returned? And the next night and the next night and the next? One simple decision could become a lifetime commitment. And did I even have the right to do it? What would the parishioners say? Or the bishop? Or the neighbors?

Father Charles at Holy Name Catholic Church in East Nashville, where he was pastor from 1977 to 1987.

Yet I decided it was the only thing to do. Like Scarlett O'Hara, I found myself saying, "I'll worry about that tomorrow."

What was on my mind in the moment was more critical. Before my very eyes were people at risk of freezing to death. It made a difference that they were just outside, underneath my window. There were others down the street on the riverbanks, in the city's vacated buildings, or hovering over the sidewalk grates, but I could not see them. Somehow, it's different when suffering people aren't right before us. It's easier to think they're someone else's problem. But that night these human beings were no one's problem but mine.

I had room and I invited them in. And they stayed the winter. They also brought others with them. And we just took every day as it came. To use Mama's expression, which I found myself doing all the time, we "put the big pot in the little pot!"

Within a week, other groups began to help. A friend from the Salvation Army arranged for cots, blankets, and some staff; a number of church groups from around East Nashville brought in food every evening; and some of our parishioners began helping regularly.

By the spring of 1986, there were enough people involved in Holy Name's "shelter" to keep it running year-round.

Those last months of 1985 into the first months of 1986, we helped a small number of unhoused people each night in East Nashville. Still, huge crowds remained out in the cold across the city. It occurred to me that if additional churches were to open their doors in a collaborative effort, we could have a much bigger impact. Nashville is known as "the city of steeples." We had the capacity if we joined together in offering hospitality. Just as we had done at Holy Name, each house of worship could create, within its own facility, a small shelter for twelve to fifteen people. By doing so, congregations would be putting into practice the words they preached.

It seemed like a workable idea and a simple one at that. It would be cost effective and yet could have a lasting impact on the lives of so many. I imagined what would happen if people of faith put their minds and hearts into it. Maybe some of the people they served would even be able to get off the streets permanently.

Thus began Room In The Inn.

EDITORS' NOTE: *Throughout his life, Charlie was a visible and vocal supporter of organizations across the city that served the marginalized.*

In addition to founding the Loaves and Fishes Community Meal in 1983 and Room In The Inn in 1986, Charlie helped spin off from Room In The Inn a homeless shelter for working men, Matthew 25, in 1987; and in 1990, he helped Winnie McKenzie organize St. Patrick's Family Shelter, which is now Safe Haven Family Shelter. He also played a role in organizing the Nashville Association of Rabbis, Priests and Ministers; the East Nashville Cooperative Ministry; the Urban Ministers Coalition; and Second Harvest Food Bank.

In 1994, three Nashville congregations—Immanuel Baptist Church, St. George's Episcopal Church, and The Temple Congregation Ohabai Sholom—came together to launch the Boulevard Bolt, a five-mile "turkey trot" on Thanksgiving morning. All proceeds from the Boulevard Bolt, now totaling millions, go to organizations that support the unhoused. Every year, Charlie was a fixture at the finish line, holding aloft a large piece of cardboard on which he'd scrawled with a Sharpie, "Thank You for Helping the Homeless."

Charlie standing at the finish line of the Boulevard Bolt, Nashville's turkey trot to benefit the unhoused, holding one of his famous handmade "Thank you for helping the homeless" signs.

The end of 1986 brought terrible tragedy. I will tell you more about it and about how the homeless saved me when I was at the lowest point in my life. Not coincidentally, the end of 1986 also marked a surge of support for Room In The Inn.

Initially, four congregations committed to shelter homeless people through March 1987. By the end of that winter, thirty-one congregations had joined. The following winter, seventy-seven congregations were involved. Now, in a typical year, Room In The Inn partners with more than one hundred congregations representing many faith traditions, college campuses, community groups, and thousands of volunteers helping to shelter thousands of their neighbors from November through March.

In addition to the winter shelter program, Room In The Inn is Nashville's only comprehensive, year-round, single site of services for individuals experiencing homelessness, where they can connect to a wide array of wrap-around services that address their multi-faceted needs and provide much-needed stability in their lives. Room In The Inn's programs offer crisis support and long-term solutions focused on four areas: Health, Education, Income, and Housing.

What started with me handing out my first peanut butter and jelly sandwich outside Holy Name's rectory door in 1977 has turned into a permanent commitment by so many to care for so many.

I would like to tell you about some of them, both the servants who have provided hospitality, safety, and a sense of belonging; and the guests who have experienced communion and community.

The first person I'd like to tell you about is Michael Hodges because he was among those first guests that freezing cold night in 1985.

He went by "Bear" and he was a veteran. Bear lived down on the east bank of the Cumberland River and was considered the mayor of the riverbank—a latter day Clayton Massie. The shanties that made up Bear's community were being torn down by the city, which was what led Bear and his friends to Holy Name's parking lot and into my line of sight.

Several years later, Room In The Inn helped get Bear into permanent housing and off the streets. I never forgot Bear over the years because I saw him as responsible for our beginnings. I often thought that, had Bear never camped out in our parking lot, Room In The Inn might never have come to be.

On September 15, 2010, Bear died of liver cancer with a roof over his head. He is buried in the Veterans Cemetery in Pegram, Tennessee.

> Blessed are the homeless. They deserve to be here.

Throughout the decades at Room In The Inn, countless grace-filled people like Bear entered my life and gave me Beatitude Moments that have never left me. What follows are the stories of several others, who represent more than I can count.

19

Madeleine DeMoss

MADELEINE'S STORY IS MORE CLOSELY ENTWINED with the success of Room In The Inn than anyone I know. She was a Holy Name parishioner and she volunteered to help the very first night we opened. Her involvement led to her becoming our first full-time staff member. She worked at Room In The Inn for twenty years until she retired. She performed every task and offered every service. She helped thousands of people over the years, yet never sought anything for herself.

Like Mama cared for us, Madeleine cared for our guests in all ways imaginable. From counseling and chastising to hugging and wiping away tears, she was a rock of security that thousands of people came to depend on.

Her memories of her time at Room In The Inn are rich in detail and full of love. These are Madeleine's own words:

> I remember my very first night, after some church service, Charlie asked if I would come and help. Two men had been fighting, and one had cut the other with a knife. His thumb was split open; I could see bone. Charlie asked, "Can you do something with his thumb?"
>
> "No doctor, no doctor!" the man shouted. The two men were Cuban boat people who had been released from the prisons and asylums under Castro. I fixed the thumb the best I could.

Madeleine DeMoss during the early days of Room In The Inn.

I remember terrible smells that I had to work hard to get past. Charlie used lots of incense to cover the odor of people who hadn't bathed in who knows how long. Holy Name didn't have showers; very few places that offered shelter had them back then. He didn't want the odor seeping into the sanctuary because he knew some parishioners might start objecting to housing the homeless.

I remember Sister Mary Agnes, who was a Sister of Mercy and in her seventies at the time, "stealing" food from her congregation to give to us. She raided the convent kitchen after nightfall and laughed mischievously that no one ever found out.

Sister Mary Agnes and I used to try to serve the food quickly so we could leave before the men took their shoes off. They had no personal hygiene opportunities.

Back then, I would go home and use Q-tips, saturated in alcohol, to clean my nostrils to get the odor out. I remember how foul the smell was. Nothing like sour, unwashed feet!

I remember Craighead's feet. He would come in and insist on taking his shoes off. I'd say, "No, Craighead!" But he kept on. I remember his feet were the worst I had ever seen. He had lost some toes to frostbite, and others were gnarled and full of blisters and sores.

In the beginning, I never really got to know the guys like I did later on.

I was task-oriented at first, and now I realize what I missed. The tasks were necessary and still are. But our volunteers have a choice: they can do tasks and we need that, but they receive a greater blessing when they try to get to know the guests.

Looking back over old records is like looking through old pictures. You remember the name, then the face, and then you remember so many who have died. But with the tears, there is also laughter because I know that they filled up my life and never took away from it. They became like my family.

For every bad situation, there were a hundred good ones. I can't count the times when they trusted me with their hurts, sorrows, disappointments, despair, as well as their hopes, joys, and successes.

I remember Sharon and how much she would laugh. I always marveled that people whose lives were so bleak could still find joy. Sharon had so much joy about her even though she had little else.

I think of Lee who was a Vietnam vet and POW. He was such a good person but couldn't get over the war. So much had happened to his body in captivity that his mind was tortured. He walked out of our life as easily as he walked in.

Susan was a lady. She had such soft skin and was so sweet and polite. She didn't live long but did move into a house in Old Hickory before she died.

In the end, I think that all the anger I had at the beginning over the injustices that I saw have turned to tears. I worry that all my efforts didn't do a whole lot.

I often reminded Madeleine that everything she did was for the good, no matter the outcome—that the homeless are our neighbors to love not our problems to solve, as Mrs. Hopwood taught me. I often reminded myself of the same thing.

Blessed are those who give their lives to the service of others. They make an impact even if they never realize it.

20

Gwen Benford

THE POLICE OFFICER under the railroad trestle on Eighth Avenue South asked if I would be willing to claim her possessions until her family could be notified. Before us was the yellow crime scene tape marking off the spot where Gwen Benford had died while sleeping out in unseasonably cool temperatures on October 11, 2009. I remember it was a Sunday morning. Strewn before us were her few possessions and some blankets that only a few hours earlier had covered her cold, lifeless body.

The officer had stopped to rouse her and a few of her friends sleeping together under the overpass but he was unable to wake her. Several other police cars arrived, and each officer knew Gwen. Crime scene detectives arrived and gave their initial assessment that she had died of natural causes. Her body was taken to the medical examiner for an autopsy.

Natural causes seemed appropriate for Gwen. It would be hard to imagine anyone hurting her on the streets, not only because everyone who knew her loved her, but also because Gwen could take care of herself.

My thoughts turned inward—full of memories of Gwen. All of them brought me a mixture of sadness and smiles.

I wish everyone could have met Gwen. Madeleine once told me, "The greatest compliment she gave me was when she said, 'I wished you had been my Mama.'" Gwen was one of several children. She remained close with her family of origin and they loved her. Ironically, some of her family members eventually became guests of Room In The Inn, too. Gwen was only thirty-four when she died, yet we knew her almost eighteen years.

I remember the many nights she would end up sleeping on my back porch (I had moved back to Twelve-Twelve after I left Holy Name), sometimes arriving as late as 3 a.m. with a friend or two. She invariably brought her typical ruckus and commotion with her, but my sleep was too deep to get up and address the matter. Later when I would see her, I would tell her, "Gwen, you know the neighbors will start to complain if you keep doing this." She would only laugh and say, "You tell 'em I'm yours."

One night the police brought her by. They said she wanted to be taken to Father Strobel's. I said, "Oh, she meant Room In The Inn." She hollered out the window of the police car, "No, I meant your house!"

Gwen was ours in a real sense. She belonged to her own loving family and also to our community. She may have gone elsewhere at times and often struggled to find her way, but she always came around and hung out with her many friends at Room In The Inn and on the street.

I remember that Sunday morning in October and can still see the police and the homeless gathered together. I think about how all of us knew her and felt her loss—a unifying moment she created around her place of death that gave witness to our common humanity.

> Blessed are those who wish to find love and experience it in unexpected ways.

Gwen Benford with Room In The Inn staff member Jeff Moles.

21

Melvin Scates

MELVIN SPENT DECADES on the streets. In the early days, he went by the name Joe Kelly and maintained a tough exterior. Sometimes, he would pat his pocket in front of Room In The Inn staff, indicating a knife or other weapon. He was reminding us that the Room In The Inn campus was *his* territory. Melvin lived a difficult life for many years and was frequently in and out of jail.

For years, I invited Melvin to stay at Room In The Inn overnight, but each time he refused and said he would be okay. He used one expression that I will never forget. He said, "I'll be okay, but you need to take care of my people." When he said that, I thought to myself, "He needs to be involved here because he sees his life on the streets as a ministry."

One day, Melvin approached our staff members and said, "You know what? Y'all are right." He was ready to accept help. He realized he wanted to change.

While Melvin's realization was sudden, his journey to a new life was long. Transitioning away from a life on the streets is never easy and many fail in their attempts. Melvin had his ups and downs but he stuck with it. He eventually began working as a shift coordinator in the Guest House, which we created in 1991, at the request of Nashville's judicial system, to provide an alternative to jail for public intoxication and to offer recuperative care for homeless people who are medically fragile. Melvin earned his GED. He completed his deacon training and was ordained in his church. He reconciled with his son and married a

> Blessed are those who seek to change their lives. They shall experience a new birth.

Melvin Scates

beautiful wife. And miracle of miracles, after years of living on the streets, Melvin was able to purchase a home.

Even if they are able to get their lives back on track, the unhoused are almost always left out of that part of the American dream we call home ownership. But Melvin was an exception. He worked at Room In The Inn for nineteen years and was quick to give the reason for his accomplishments. "God blessed me," he said, "and Room In The Inn planted the seeds of that blessing." He also credited his pastor and members of his church, as well as his realtor and mortgage broker, both of whom he met when they served as volunteers for Room In The Inn's winter shelter program.

Melvin's support system represented that broader circle of people that defines our sense of family, our experience of community, and our appreciation of feeling at home. Melvin's story reminds us how important the support of others is in accomplishing anything in life.

For many years until his death, Melvin continued to work full-time at the Guest House to pay it forward. He helped hundreds of others who shared his early experiences move toward better lives.

EDITORS' NOTE: *Melvin died on March 10, 2023, two days before Charlie's eightieth birthday and five months before Charlie's own death. Along with the entire Room In The Inn community, Charlie mourned Melvin deeply.*

22

Rachel Hester

RACHEL'S STORY IS ONE of great commitment and spirit. A preacher's daughter, she came to Room In The Inn in 1989 as a young volunteer in college. Most congregations initially knew her as the coordinator of Room In The Inn's winter shelter program. But over the years, she learned every facet of the organization and eventually became Executive Director of Room In The Inn in 2005.

Rachel Hester (third from right) and Charlie Strobel (second from left) surrounded by guests of Room In The Inn.

Rachel is extremely creative and smart and brings tremendous energy and passion, often with a great sense of humor, to everything she touches. She approaches her work with a contagious, joyful spirit. Rachel has been a great leader who has won the respect of all. She has overseen the expansion of Room In The Inn's facilities to a total of 64,000 square feet. Our current multi-million dollar, five-story addition includes three floors of affordable housing.

She and Room In The Inn's staff are now poised to complete more upcoming expansions, thus increasing Room In The Inn's ability to effectively serve Nashville's most vulnerable residents.

> Blessed are those who have great potential,
> for they will be discovered.

EDITORS' NOTE: *Rachel wrote the following remembrance about her first encounter with Charlie, which was printed in the Room In The Inn newsletter published in Fall 2023 just after Charlie died:*

I first met Charlie Strobel in 1989 when I was a college freshman, new to Nashville. My church was a Room In The Inn congregation and my job was to "offer hospitality" to the guests we hosted every Thursday evening. Each week, I showed up to do my part. But that Thanksgiving, I arrived and the fellowship hall was dark. The beds were not set up, the food was still in the freezer. No one else arrived to help. I called Room In The Inn to cancel.

Charlie answered the phone. I explained our situation and thought that would be the end of the conversation. Instead, it was the beginning of the rest of my life.

For every logistical problem I presented, Charlie had a solution. I said I didn't know how to drive the bus. He told me to come pick him up, bring him back to the church and he would drive the bus. I said the food was frozen. He said he'd get some at Mrs. Winner's. He made clear to me it isn't what we have to offer that matters. It's how we make people feel. That night, Charlie broadened my view of what it really means to "offer hospitality." It means preparing our hearts as much as preparing our space. That night we all shared more than a meal. Charlie showed us—the volunteers and the guests—that we need each other.

Over the years, Charlie and I would work on incredibly complex issues together. Issues involving broken systems crushing already broken people. The more daunting the issue, the more Charlie would elevate the simple biblical precept to love our neighbor. If we can do nothing else, he said, we must welcome our guests—just as they are. Charlie recognized that those we served had fallen out of the very systems created to protect all of us—education, health care, mental health, employment, housing, family and even religion. He believed that making room in our lives for all people and circumstances made room for God.

Charlie also believed people are good. All people. His confidants and coworkers included those of every race, ethnicity, generation, gender and faith practice. He believed spending time with people who were different and thought differently than he did was the best way to reach creative and lasting solutions to injustice.

In conveying his belief in each person's fundamental goodness, Charlie brought out the best in everyone he touched.

Photo of the first stand-alone Room In The Inn location in downtown Nashville, taken in 1995.

The Room In The Inn campus in downtown Nashville, built in 2010.

PART V
The Miracle of Forgiveness

23

Billy Denton

> "If only it were all so simple! If only there were evil people somewhere insidiously committing evil deeds, and it were necessary only to separate them from the rest of us and destroy them. But the line dividing good and evil cuts through the heart of every human being. And who is willing to destroy a piece of his own heart?"
>
> —ALEKSANDR SOLZHENITSYN

BILLY DENTON HAD a Mickey Mouse clock radio. Every morning when that radio rang, Billy bolted awake and rushed outside to the front porch next door to meet up with me, his good friend.

This was a daily ritual, and if Mickey Mouse didn't do his job, I returned the favor, rushing over to Billy's front porch. For three years as next-door neighbors growing up in North Nashville, we spent as much time as possible together. We made no decisions without consulting each other. Every day, we explored the world of possibilities. From going to the ballfield to watching a movie together to working on our bicycle brakes and hundreds of other experiences, every day was an adventure. We filled each other's space and discovered the world around us.

But things weren't perfect. Inevitably, there were conflicts between us, for that's part of the nature of friendships. Initially, the conflicts did not seem that important. But over time, they began to escalate, which concerned many adults around us, particularly Mama.

Billy grew out his fingernails, and when we fought, he would scratch me. On one occasion, he scratched my face so badly he left a lifelong scar below my left eye. Mama was upset. Prone to hyperbole as she was, she said, "You'd better quit fighting! Y'all are going to kill each other!"

But I was angry. I told myself, "I'm not going to let Billy get away with that." So the next time we were rolling around in the grass and the dirt, I got on top of Billy, put my hands around his throat and started choking him until his face became blood red. I don't remember exactly how old I was—maybe seven or eight. But my memory of doing this is as strong as my memory of my father's body at the funeral home and of Mr. Orskiborsky's room at the Buddeke House. I remember thinking to myself, "I can kill him." And that scared me. I immediately let go, Billy got up, and life went on.

Eventually, Billy's family moved across town, and we lost touch. But I never forgot my first best friend—or the terrifying realization of what I was capable of as I loomed over him with my hands around his neck.

Later, when people talked with me about capital punishment and said, "I could never kill anybody," I knew better. I would tell them, "Yes, you could. I know what it means to be pushed to the point of committing life-altering violence." While I realize I was a small child at the time, I instinctively understood in that moment Solzhenitsyn's words, *But the line dividing good and evil cuts through the heart of every human being.* I experienced that with Billy Denton.

I have often wondered about anger and conflict, and why they escalate. I suspect it comes from nursing grudges and holding on to one another's mistakes. In a thousand little ways, we do not forgive. Rather than holding the secrets of others, we hold their sins.

We do this when we know someone has done something wrong—it can be a slight indiscretion or a serious evil—and we let it lodge in our minds and fester. We always see the person who has done the wrong through the lens of their mistake and can't let it go.

It reminds me of the story of Jesus not only forgiving the woman charged with adultery but bringing her accusers up short. As the crowd was preparing to stone her to death, Jesus said, "Let the one who is without sin cast the first stone." Everyone wandered away until there was no one left to hold the woman's sin anymore. Then Jesus said to the woman, "Who is there to accuse you?" She said, "No one, Lord." And he said, "Neither do I. Now go and sin no more."

This story and the story of Jesus' death give us all permission to think and act in the same way—to say to one another, "Go in peace." Though Jesus dies, he leaves a legacy of forgiveness, of letting people go into their future with hope.

His is a love that is stronger than death, a love that never dies.

Jesus invites us into a world without condemnation. He calls us to call others into that same world. The disciples hear him say, "Receive the Holy Spirit. Whose sins you shall forgive they are forgiven, whose sins you shall retain, they are retained." The choice now becomes ours. We can hold each other in our mistakes, or we can let each other go. We can be a prison to one another or the source of release. Both are choices. One leads us to separation; the other leads us to communion.

> Blessed are they who love their neighbors and hold their secrets, for they shall find forgiveness.

The greatest sin that society holds on to is the taking of human life—to the point that we sanction the murder of murderers.

When I was a student at Catholic University, the topic of capital punishment arose. I remember discussing in moral theology classes every possible moral issue you could imagine: war, racism, poverty, murder, rape, totalitarianism, abortion, euthanasia, lying, cheating and stealing. Capital punishment was among them.

I can remember discussing the pros and cons of this issue and concluding that I was against it on two levels: both my reason and my gut feelings were against killing even a killer.

Inevitably, the question would always arise in our discussions, "Would you change your opinion if it affected you personally, due to a crime against you or a member of your own family?" I remember just as clearly saying in the objectivity of that classroom that I hoped I would not change my mind about capital punishment, even if it affected me personally.*

Never in my wildest imagination did I foresee that this hypothetical case would become my reality, and I would one day have to face that choice.

---

* In 1977, Charlie testified before the Tennessee General Assembly in opposition to the death penalty. Mindful that he could not know the pain of those who had suffered the murder of a loved one, he nonetheless said he hoped he would stand against the death penalty even if his own family member were murdered.

24

Antony and Cleopatra

ON THE COLD AFTERNOON of December 10, 1986, I was coming off the altar at Holy Name after saying 5:30 p.m. Mass when I received a call from my sister, Veronica.

She asked, "Have you seen Mama?" I said, "No." She said, "Well, we can't find her anywhere."

We called friends and family together to try to find her. I drove all around the city for hours with my brother Jerry, my brother-in-law Tom Seigenthaler, and a family friend named Bill Hamlin, who was a lieutenant with the Metro Nashville Police Department and a Holy Name parishioner. Not long after midnight on December 11, we finally spotted her car parked in the Nashville Rescue Mission parking lot, across the street from the Greyhound bus station. But Mama was nowhere to be found.

Soon, more police officers arrived, and they asked us for a spare key to her car. One among our group went to get it. I stayed in the Union Rescue Mission parking lot with the police.

I vividly remember two things as we were all standing there waiting for the key. The first was that Mama wasn't the neatest person and never washed her car, yet there was a big clean swipe across the trunk that someone had made. The second was that, at some point, a police officer walked over to the back of her car, placed his foot on the bumper and pushed down, as if testing the weight of the contents of the trunk. Both these things gave me a terrible feeling.

Mary Catherine Strobel surrounded by her children, Alice, Charles, Jerry, and Veronica, in December 1985, the Christmas before she was killed.

Once we provided the spare key, the officers opened the car's trunk. Inside was my Mama, nestled there like a little baby. She had been stabbed to death.

An investigation immediately followed but turned up no suspects. We held a funeral for Mary Catherine Schweiss Strobel on December 13, 1986, at the Assumption. It drew more than one thousand mourners. Her inexplicable murder shocked the city and brought forth a profound outpouring of love and appreciation from the Nashville community she had cherished.

What follows is an excerpt from the eulogy I delivered that day:

In Shakespeare's play *Antony and Cleopatra*, Cleopatra says to Antony as he dies, with all of the anguish and heartache in her soul:

"Noblest of men, would you die? Have you no care of me?
Shall I live in this dull world, which in your absence is no better
than a sty?"

Until early Thursday morning, none of us knew how painfully empty Mama must have felt when Daddy died thirty-nine years ago, December 21, 1947. In her eyes and in the eyes of those who knew him, he was the noblest of men, her source of life and love.

When Daddy died, she gathered us together and kneeling around his bed, said, "God is going to help us, your Daddy will always be there to watch over us, and we need to stay together." Then we said the rosary.

Two days later, after the family had returned from the cemetery, a call came from a woman whose friend had a little baby who was dying. She needed Mama. So Mama left her house full of company, her children, her own grief, and went to the woman and child.

I think it's important to understand that in the handling of the events of my Daddy's death, Mama was teaching us a lesson for us to learn today. And that lesson has two parts.

The first part is this:

1) As devastating and as empty as her death is to us—and it is the hardest thing we have ever done—we must paraphrase her words. "God is going to help us, our Mama will always be there to watch over us, and we need to stay together."

The second lesson is this:

2) Now two days later, as we return to our homes, there will still be great, great needs all around us, and we must try to respond to them as she would want us to. "It can be done," she says. "It must be done," she says.

Many have said that she did not deserve to die the way that she did. Yet for years, we have heard it said that "God did not spare his only Son but delivered him up, and the Son emptied himself and humbled himself, obediently accepting even death, death on a cross." In Mama's death, our family believes that the viciousness inflicted on such gentleness and kindness, as was her way, brings about a great *communion* with Jesus.

So, how can we question its course? It seems to run true to the form of Jesus's own death. And why speak of anger and revenge? Those words are not compatible with the very thought of our Mother.

So, I say to everyone: We are not angry or vengeful, just deeply hurt. And you and many others have helped to ease our pain.

We know the answers are not easy and clear. But we still believe in the miracle of forgiveness . . . and extend our arms in that embrace."*

---

* See Appendix A for the full eulogy.

My mother lived a life of tireless, joyful service to her community and particularly to those in need: the poor, the sick, the homeless, and the helpless. She came to see everyone she encountered as "family" and never met a stranger.

As a very young child, she would ask her father for money to buy food for poor neighbors and collected useful items to deliver around the neighborhood. Mama's approach to giving throughout her life was exclusively hands on. Her car was a rolling general store with supplies of food, clothes, funeral wreaths, shoes, books, newspapers for paper drives, and other goods for those in need. Her typical day—and the day she died started out as a typical day—might involve visiting several hospitals, assisting at a soup kitchen, attending a funeral, and taking clothing to people in need, whom she always referred to as "my friends." She gave her greatest gifts freely: her time, her love, her faith, and her good humor.

Two days after Mama died, my family released a statement, which read in part:

> Perhaps, it is the irony of God that a woman who abhorred violence died so violently, that a woman who gave so much to the needy lost her life in the act of serving them.
>
> No horror can change our belief that the concern and love that our mother meant to us and to so many others is the best response to the violence and disregard we see around us all in the world.*

Mama was murdered one year after I looked out my bedroom window in the rectory of Holy Name, saw people sleeping in the bitter cold, and invited them in.

Room In The Inn as a citywide program of shelter and hospitality was just getting underway when she died. In one sense, I had no choice but to go on. As I said in my eulogy at her funeral, I felt bound to respond to the great, great needs all around me, as she had done.

But in another—and much more profound—sense, the homeless saved my life. As I have recounted many times, I was curled up in the fetal position after Mama died. And I heard, metaphorically, their voices saying, "Get up. Open the gate." I didn't want to. I was destroyed. But I got up. I opened the gate.

The city of Nashville got up with me. Room In The Inn's first winter shelter

---

* See Appendix B for the full statement.

program launched in November of 1986 with only four congregations. By March of 1987, four months after Mama's death, our number was thirty-one.

I've always believed that Mama had a hand in our early success. She had a way of reaching people. She believed everyone was good.

It has been my experience, as I have asked time and time again for support for the unhoused from individuals, congregations of every denomination, and organizations of every kind, that Mama was right.

> Blessed are those who see the best in everyone. Their memories will bring even more good to the world.

EDITORS' NOTE: *Charles's sister Alice recalls that Charles always called her on December 9, the anniversary of their mother's murder:*

Every year Charles called to check on me, asking gently, "How are you doing?" I'd tell him I was okay, just missing Mama so much. He would agree, saying, "I know, I miss her too."

Then we would relive the horrible nightmare: our last day spent with Mama; our memorable conversations; our confusion on December 10 when we couldn't find her; our despair when checking with family, friends, and local hospitals and realizing no one had seen her; our utter shock and heartbreaking grief when the unthinkable happened—Mama's lifeless body was discovered in the trunk of her car.

Our conversation on Mama's death anniversary was like a much-needed therapy session for both of us. After a good cry and a few laughs about some funny Mama memories, we always ended with, "I love you."

I missed his call on December 9, 2023, and will for the rest of my days as I adjust to life without Charles.

25

The Murderer

AFTER MAMA'S DEATH, I made significant changes in my life. I decided to take a leave of absence from the priesthood and devote myself full-time to working with the homeless. Bishop Niedergeses told me I needed to find a priest to replace me at Holy Name in order to take the leave. I asked my dear friend Joe Sanches, whom I'd met during my years at the Theological College at Catholic U., to serve as the pastor during my absence. Joe sought and received permission from his order to support me—and ended up serving Holy Name for decades.

I would eventually return to active ministry. But during those initial years after Mama died, I was driven by both grief and passion. I had to do what I felt I was meant to do with my life.

Also very soon after she died, I was presented with another problem I felt I was being called to address. The problem of capital punishment.

One month after Mama's funeral, we learned she had been abducted by a man named William Scott Day, who had escaped from a psychiatric prison in the Midwest a few days before he crossed her path.

Law enforcement apprehended Day on January 14, 1987, in the small town of Van Horn, Texas, where he'd been caught driving a car stolen from another innocent victim he'd killed. After his arrest, Day willingly confessed to murdering six people during his thirty-nine days of freedom. Mama was the first.

Day gave a detailed account of what he'd done to her. He told police he had made his way to Nashville on a bus and was casing the parking lot of the Sears store near the Greyhound station downtown, looking for someone to rob and a car to steal. Mama happened to be leaving the Sears store right about this time. Later, after Nashville officers had meticulously reconstructed the events of her day on December 9, we would learn she'd gone to Sears to get her watch repaired, one of many mundane errands and errands of mercy she'd performed in the hours before William Scott Day spotted her moving toward her car as the sun was going down on that cold afternoon.

The photo Mary Catherine's family shared with media in the wake of her murder on December 9, 1986.

As Mama approached the driver-side door, Day, who was well over six feet tall, set upon her with a small knife in his hand and put it to her throat. He forced her into the passenger seat of her car, then drove her around for three hours before murdering her and stuffing her in the trunk. Police would later find the contents of the trunk, including provisions for the poor, on the ground near the spot where Day killed her. He'd dumped them out to make room for her body. Day then abandoned her car and her body in the parking lot of the Union Rescue Mission, which was located next door to the Greyhound station, before fleeing Nashville on another bus and continuing with his murder spree.

At around 1 a.m. on the morning of December 11, after we'd scoured the city for hours looking for her, we finally spotted her car, unmistakable with its license plate reading, "Let Me Tell You About My Grandchildren." Our lives would never be the same.

On January 16, 1987, hours after learning of Day's confession from Metro Nashville police who'd traveled to Van Horn to interview him, my family released a second statement:

> Today, we are facing the incomplete news accounts that a suspect has been arrested in the death of our mother, Mary Catherine Strobel, and in the deaths of six other persons.*

We know the deep hurt those other families are suffering. We pray that God's consolation and the love of their families and friends will strengthen them.

Future investigations will expose the horrible circumstances of our mother's death. The cruelty of her death, as devastating as it is, does not diminish our belief that God's forgiveness and love, as our mother showed us, is the only response to the violence we know.

If this suspect is guilty as alleged, it is clear to us that he is deeply troubled and needs all the compassion that our society and its institutions can offer.

Soon after William Scott Day's arrest, the Nashville district attorney announced his intention to seek the death penalty. My family met with him and expressed our opposition to this decision. We believed we had to speak out. If not, our silence would give consent and acceptance of society's unwritten rule of returning violence with violence. At the time, I wrote:

> I believe that we need to petition the district attorney not to seek the death penalty for William Scott Day, accused of murdering our Mother. I believe we need to say, "Spare his life." Enough is enough. I can think of no way that his execution would bring us satisfaction.
>
> Besides the appeal we make in this community for his life, I think that we believe in one another as members of a family that has been taught from our ancestors the beauty and value of human life. We now inherit that tradition and want to pass it on to our children and to their children and to their children. I hope that ages from now our family descendants will look back at our actions and understand that in an age of vengeance, we chose not to be vengeful but tried to be faithful to our most cherished family teaching, namely, that God is love itself, has given us his life generously, yes, even unto death, and expects nothing less from us.
>
> In my mind, William Scott Day is a child of God, created in the image of God, and loved by God. Can we think of him in any other way? In the destiny of God, he is forever linked to us and has become a part of us and we a part of him.
>
> I believe that our words of forgiveness are only symbolic if we do not use every opportunity within the system to prevent his execution.

---

* This statement, written in the immediate aftermath of Day's confession when details were still unclear, is factually inaccurate. Day killed six people in total—Mary Catherine Strobel and five others.

In the aftermath of his mother's murder, Charlie advocated against the death penalty.

> Finally, I want the court to give him the maximum number of years for the protection of society.*

Ultimately, Day received three consecutive life sentences, but was not sentenced to death. He died of natural causes on February 4, 2006, at the West Tennessee State Penitentiary. When I heard the news that Day had died, I found my reaction interesting. I wasn't angry, and I didn't feel in my heart that justice had finally been done. Probably the closest I could come to identifying how I reacted was sadness, because he had ruined so much of our lives—and the lives of his own family, too.

Even after this deeply painful experience, my opinion still has not changed. My family and I still say what we expressed in December 1986: "We know the answers are not easy and clear, but we still believe in the miracle of forgiveness and extend our arms in that embrace."

"The miracle of forgiveness." Even though we said it, we never knew the consequences that were to follow. But these are the things we learned:

1. **FORGIVENESS BRINGS PEACE.** The person who killed our mother forced an evil on our hearts. Stamping out the killer doesn't stamp out the evil. It's done. We understand how painful it can be, and we understand the feeling

---

* See Appendix C for the full statement.

of others that this person deserved to die for killing someone we loved so much. But it wouldn't even the score. You can never even the score by killing anyone or even killing a thousand. For what remains is a broken heart that cannot find peace. Forgiving the killer heals the heart and brings peace. A wonderful, unexpected peace.

2. **FORGIVENESS RESTORES A PROPER SENSE OF JUSTICE.** Every life has supreme value. Every life. God does not make exceptions. We are taught that God is the author of life and death. When a killer takes the life of another, that person mistakenly assumes a power reserved only for God, and the proper sense of justice is destroyed in that act. Forgiveness affirms once again a belief in the justice of God, and punishment without execution keeps our society from making the same mistake about justice that the killer has made.

3. **FORGIVENESS BRINGS FREEDOM.** As long as revenge remains in our hearts, we are enslaved. Enslaved to the mind of the killer. He lives inside us. The killer's motives and actions consume our own heart. They control us. We remain stuck there forever in the events and circumstances of the murder. Forgiveness frees us from the killer's grip on our hearts—from the killer's motivation and deeds—and allows us to be free of his control over us. Forgiveness brings closure to a traumatic situation and frees us to begin to take the small, painful, day-by-day steps to go on with our lives.

Although these reflections remain true for me, they don't compare to the simple, yet profound reason Mama gave me. Once, I asked her how she felt about capital punishment. And she paused a bit before she answered. Then she said something that only a parent can appreciate. She said, "Well, I wouldn't want it to happen to you." For her it was that simple. If she couldn't allow it to happen to her own child, how could she allow it for anyone's child?

> Blessed are those who forgive, for they shall
> find freedom, justice, and peace.

26

The Japanese

I BELIEVE FORGIVENESS IS INTEGRAL to building communities of nonviolence that radiate love and respect. Like so many of the things I understand to be true, this awareness came to me as a young child.

I was born in 1943 into a world at war. Following the attack on Pearl Harbor on December 7, 1941, my family heard frightening words from President Franklin D. Roosevelt about it being "a date which will live in infamy." The bombing turned the axis powers, led by Germany and Japan, into enemies of the United States. Countless lives were lost.

Until the war ended on September 2, 1945, the city of Nashville and the nation were virulently anti-Japanese and spoke of them in extremely derogatory terms. Imagine a headline three inches high on the front page of the *Nashville Banner,* the city's afternoon newspaper, that blared a message from the publisher to "destroy the yellow-bellied, slant-eyed" Japanese army.

In my own neighborhood, which was heavily populated by people of German ancestry, hatred of the Japanese was strong, maybe even stronger than other places. This likely was an attempt at deflection. Anti-German sentiment also ran high during the war, so people with German backgrounds broadcast their loyalty to the United States by vilifying the Japanese and talking about them as if they were subhuman.

As a very young child, I must have been around a lot of ugly talk about "Japs" and this apparently bothered me, according to what Mama told me later. I began to feel sorry for the Japanese who were hated and being killed, and I was upset that people in my world seemed happy about it.

Mama said I wanted a security blanket, like Linus in "Peanuts." She and Daddy gave me a stuffed doll that I slept with every night, and Mama said I had a name for it. I called it "Jap." She said I wouldn't go anywhere—to church, to the grocery store, to visit relatives—without taking my friend "Jap" with me. She also said that I was the only one in the household who used that name; "Japs" were the enemy and the word was a slur. Well-meaning adults tried to talk me into calling my doll something else, but I insisted on protecting and defending my little friend "Jap."

I'm not sure why I wanted and needed to create a friend whose name was synonymous with evil during those difficult years. But I'd like to think that in some subconscious way, I was trying to practice what was being preached to me: that hatred and violence are wrong and self-defeating, and that we are called to love our supposed enemies. I suspect I was getting conflicting messages during this time of war, because my parents and aunts were peace-loving people, and I was trying to work it out.

I do know I carried this understanding of the futility of violence into adulthood, as did my siblings. We made this clear in our statement asking that the man who killed our mother not be killed in her name.

Over the years I've expressed my belief in the power of nonviolence in many settings. I've also supported the Catholic bishops and popes in opposing war. And I've always mourned on August 6, 1945, the day the allies dropped an atomic bomb on Hiroshima.* The scars of that bombing ended the war but did not bring about peace. Today, we still live under that first nuclear cloud and continue to wage war that has expanded into terrorism, atrocities, riots, and violence worldwide.

Yet I maintain my belief that it doesn't have to be this way, and I do not think my faith in peace is either childish or naïve. Room In The Inn is my case in point.

I remember the beginnings of Room In The Inn when there were fights almost nightly. The fights were happening at our central gathering place, not at the congregations where homeless people were being taken for a meal and to

---

* Charles died on August 6, the same day as the bombing he commemorated every year.

spend the night. Most of the fights were over seemingly isolated issues—someone was pushed inadvertently, a bag was stolen, a guy got in front of another guy in line, someone called another person a name. The very first fight was over a cigarette.

But these matters were not minor to the people involved. Those who came to our central location were angry enough over having little or nothing. The end of the day, which was when they gathered at Room In The Inn, had usually brought no job and no breaks; all they wanted was something to eat. Instead, they found themselves in a large crowd of one hundred to two hundred people and still one step away from a meal and a bed for the night. When the indignity of being disrespected was added to the mix, people began to push and shove. Often, jostling led to an explosion. It was like handling dynamite.

I would jump into the middle of the mix as quickly as I could when these fights started to try to keep both parties apart. When I succeeded, I tried, just as quickly, to take those involved to a back room to talk and settle things. Meanwhile, the crowd that had circled those who were fighting watched and wondered what was going to happen. In some strange and sad way, this was a form of entertainment for them. It also was a reminder to me of how acclimated they were to life in a violent world.

I don't remember having a lot of concrete solutions for resolving the fights that happened in those early days, except to claim one principle consistently: the principle of *respect*. Before things returned to "normal," everyone had to hear me preach about love and respect for each other. I can't count the number of times I repeated after every fight, "We have to take care of each other. No one else will or even cares. I don't blame you if you're mad. Nobody should have to live like this. Everyone deserves better than this. But we're all we've got tonight. We need each other."

As the years passed, fewer and fewer fights occurred. Everyone came to understand that violence accomplished nothing other than unloading a lot of anger and causing some serious pain. The guests of Room In The Inn also learned not to leave resolution of conflicts to law enforcement. Usually, by the time the police were called and responded, we were already cleaning up the blood. In time, everybody began to realize that there was no need to call the police, that people should be able to resolve their differences reasonably.

Today there are rarely violent outbursts at Room In The Inn. This is not to say

Charlie and Room In The Inn volunteers gear up before the nightly winter shelter program.

there are no moments of tension or legitimate grievances. We experience such moments. But both participants and staff call on each other to respect one another in dealing with conflict. Everyone who participates in Room In The Inn wants it to be a place of *sanctuary* and does their part to make it so.

Our mission statement expresses our six core values: *Through the power of spirituality and the practice of love, Room In The Inn provides hospitality with a respect that offers hope in a community of nonviolence.*

The world of the homeless is filled with hatred and violence. Everyone at Room In The Inn does whatever we can to create sanctuary. We start by defining violence as four types of abuse: *physical, verbal, racial,* and *sexual.*

In our Room In The Inn orientation, we identify these four types of abuse and establish rights and responsibilities to combat them, each one rooted in respect. They exist to protect each guest, staff member, and volunteer and to ensure the program runs smoothly—all within an atmosphere free of violence.*

The normal response to violence is to rely on the discipline and protection of the law. Yet we at Room In The Inn understand that legal protections are limited and do not always bring justice. The unhoused are used to injustice. This

---

* Detailed rights and responsibilities are listed in Appendix D.

leads to a tendency to "take the law into your own hands," since many come to believe they should not have to suffer injustice passively.

But Room In The Inn's ethos is not passive. It is an active force rooted in love and respect. And it is countercultural. Unlike the values of "might makes right" that prevail in too many communities and on the streets, a nonviolent community believes that love disarms conflicts, de-escalates violence, and diffuses hatred.

To be clear, Room In The Inn is not free of violence out of fear of violence. We subscribe to Dr. Martin Luther King Jr.'s six Principles of Nonviolence, the first of which asserts, "Nonviolence is a way of life for courageous people."[*]

The sanctuary we provide remains one of Room In The Inn's greatest achievements and lessons—namely, that people of diverse backgrounds can live together in peace and resolve their differences through reasonable dialogue, not force.

> Blessed are they who desire a world of peace, for they shall achieve it.

---

[*] All of Dr. King's Principles of Nonviolence are listed in Appendix E.

PART VI

Getting Ready to Die

Father Dan and Father Charles at the Assumption for Charles's First Mass, February 1, 1970.

⚜ 27 ⚜

The Pastor

WHEN I WAS A BOY growing up on Seventh Avenue North, the Church of the Assumption served an older population and there were a lot of funerals. We lived so close to the church that Father Dan often called my brother Jerry and me to be acolytes for these funerals. I served more of them than I can count and at every funeral Father Dan preached the same sermon. Prince or pauper, everybody heard these words: "We're on this earth to get ready to die."

I tell this story to a lot of people, and some have said it sounds so morbid. But that's not how the parish heard Father Dan's words. Our pastor was helping us see death in the context of our whole life's journey to God. And what better time to talk about this than when the body of the deceased was right in front of us.

After asserting, "We're on this earth to get ready to die," Father Dan then said, "And when we die, God is not going to say, '[John, Joe, Mary, Sue,] What did you do for a living? How much money did you make? How many friends did you have?' God is only going to ask us two questions: 'Did you love me?' and 'Did you love your neighbor?' And we know that [John, Joe, Mary, Sue] will answer truthfully, saying, 'Yes, Lord, you know I loved you. You know I loved my neighbor.' And then God will say, 'Well, done, good and faithful servant. Enter now into the joy of the Lord.'"

Father Dan had a soft voice and his delivery was perfect. He nailed his funeral sermon every single time. Even though I knew exactly what was coming, he always made me cry. I never heard his words as anything but positive and hopeful: we come from God and we return to God, so death was never frightening to me.

One day, Father Dan's own time came to return to God. In June of 1995, I got a call from his caregiver, Martha, who told me he might not make it through the night. "If you want to see him," she said, "this is the best time to come."

He was lying in bed when I arrived. I pulled up a chair to be as close to him as I could. I leaned in and said, "Father Dan, this is Charles. I hope you can hear me. I'm here to do two things.

"First, I want to tell you how much you have meant to my family and to thank you for helping Mama take care of us. You were like a father to me after my own father died.

"Second, I'm here to be your priest."

Then I began: "Father Dan, soon you will face God, and God's going to ask you two questions: 'Dan, did you love me? Dan, did you love your neighbor?' We know that you can say, without hesitation, 'Yes, Lord, you know I loved you. You know I loved my neighbor.' And then you can hear God say, 'Well done, good and faithful servant. Enter now into the joy of the Lord.'"

Up to that point, I wasn't sure he was alert enough to hear me. But when I said, "Well done, good and faithful servant. Enter now into the joy of the Lord," I saw one tear roll down his cheek. And I knew that he had heard everything.

It is one of my greatest memories.

Our lives begin and end with God. But we must do all our living in between birth and death, always on a journey to return to the One who made us. The theologian John Shea calls us "Middle People" and describes all of humanity this way:

> We have no choice but to begin where we are; and where we are is in the middle. It is not given us to stand on the far side of human space, at a moment before the rush of human time and then, with all deliberation and grace, to enter. Nor is it given us to find an indisputable starting point, a Cartesian rock from which to launch understanding and action. Our first awareness is that we are swimming. We wake in the water. Our beginnings are not wholly our own. Our endings will most likely be beyond our control. We are middle people.

Father Dan said the same thing much more simply, and no less beautifully, every time he faced a church full of grieving people: we're all here getting ready to die.

And so, what does this in-between life teach us? I believe we are here to learn to live a life of love, forgiveness, and communion.

Not even Jesus is spared the mystery of death. Even though he had told his followers, "I am going to the Father . . . I go ahead of you," his disciples' loss was palpable, a physical pain. This is how deep grief over the loss of someone dear to us makes us feel. I remember this pain after Mama died. I remember wanting only to see her again and to have her tell me she wasn't suffering.

We who are left behind desperately want to stay connected. We want some indication that he is somewhere tangible or that she is at peace. We believe we will accept the loss more easily if we are reassured the person we love is happy in some other place. We look for signs that will help us move on without them.

We also imagine our loved one has gone ahead to prepare a place for us, just as Jesus told his followers he would do. We hope the ones we long for will return for us when our own time comes. We've all heard stories of someone close to death who sees visions of deceased family members hovering in the room—a sort of welcoming committee helping the dying person make the journey.

Mama loved a good party and was the head of the welcoming committee. Getting together with friends and family was her favorite way to spend time, the more the merrier. I remember her so vividly, standing by the doorway as people began to gather, clapping as they joined the festivities and calling out, "This is just like heaven's gonna be! Everybody waiting for the next one to come!"

Now that I am in the final chapter of my own life, I remember her longing for the ones she lost. My father, her aunts, her parents, and so many more who were precious to her. I remember her vision of heaven as one big family reunion with everyone eagerly awaiting the arrival of the others.

I think about them all. The Middle People, who did the best they could with the life God gave them. Mama, Daddy, Aunt Mollie, Aunt Kate, Mr. Albert, Mary Hopwood, Michael Hodges, Gwen Benford, Melvin Scates, and everyone else who helped me understand why I was born.

And I think about Father Dan, my pastor, who gave me the words for what so many taught me by example: we're on this earth to get ready to die.

> Blessed are those who grieve, for they shall one day return to God.

EDITORS' NOTE: *On Friday, August 11, 2023, Reverend Becca Stevens, Chaplain of St. Augustine's Episcopal Chapel and a longtime friend and colleague of Charlie's, gave the eulogy at a citywide gathering celebrating his life. Among many remembrances, she had this to say:*

Charlie shuffled off this mortal coil knowing it is the climax of life, not the end. He believed all our journeys begin and end with God and our job while we live is to prepare to die. So this is the requited love with his creator Charlie longed for his whole life. Selfishly I wish for one more conversation to ask him to please tell us what it is like. Instead I will have to do what Charlie always counseled, keep going and pray for a sign.

I went with Charlie to sit at more than a few deathbeds over the years. He would always offer last rites, recite the twenty-third psalm and then lean in and whisper, "Tell God I am doing the best I can." I pray that on Charlie's Easter morning he has put in a good word for us as we journey home and make our own Easter morning song, "Alleluiah, Alleluiah, Alleluiah."

28

Vince

A PORTRAIT HANGS in our Room In The Inn boardroom. In it, I am sitting next to a man who has seen hard times. He is stooped and battle-weary. His dark hair is partially covered by a rumpled hat. His jaw is slack and his hand grips a crutch. My arm is around the man's shoulder. Close by his feet, as if to warm them, is my little dog Lulabelle.*

It is a portrait of community. It is also a portrait of what was and what might have been. The man next to me was a long-time guest of Room In The Inn. He was also one of my oldest childhood friends. His name was Vince.

Vince and I attended school together, from first grade all the way through grammar school. Everyone at Assumption School generally got along, and I can still recall the names of most of my classmates: Cecilia, Paul, Jerry, Rosemary, Richard, Judy, John, Ethel, Joyce, and—of course—Vince.

Vince was part of our community, but he also had a foul mouth and a penchant for fighting and getting into trouble. The students at Assumption simply accepted him for who he was. We never expected him to be any different and we never took it personally when Vince would stir up an argument or a fight. We just viewed his behavior as part of who he was.

Vince and his family moved away around the time he started high school, just up the road in another area of North Nashville called Bordeaux. While the

---

* According to Msgr. Campion, the portrait was a gift to Charles from the Nashville Conference of Christians and Jews.

Charlie and his childhood friend Vince sit on a Room In The Inn cot with Lulabelle at their feet. This portrait now hangs in the Room In The Inn boardroom.

rest of us moved on together, attending local Catholic high schools for girls and boys, Vince went to Cumberland High School where he knew no one.

As a new student at Cumberland, Vince was no longer surrounded by the supportive community in the neighborhood where he grew up. Those of us who attended grammar school with Vince had learned to overlook a lot of his behavior, but students at Cumberland were less tolerant of him. Vince didn't change his attitude or his brash, arrogant ways at Cumberland. He continued to confront other students and instigate fights.

One day during his sophomore year, Vince got into a fight with a classmate. His teacher pulled him and the other student aside and told them they would have to settle the disagreement after school. He and the other student decided to have at each other in the school parking lot later that afternoon. From what I heard, the fight was brutal, and Vince was beaten to a pulp. His brain swelled, and he was transported to the hospital, where doctors had to perform surgery to relieve the pressure on his brain. Vince survived, but he was forever changed.

He was left with a big horseshoe-shaped scar on the side of his head and permanent brain damage.

Not long after this event, while Vince and I were still in high school, I heard that someone had run a car head on into a stone wall at the entrance to St. Cecilia Academy, one of the city's three Catholic girls schools. The impact created a six-foot hole in the wall, causing the stone to completely crumble. I learned later that Vince was driving the car. I remember thinking, "It's a wonder he's not dead."

After the collision, Vince ended up dropping out of high school. He got married and had two children, but he never held a permanent job. About four or five years later, the ramifications of Vince's brain injury caused him to have a stroke, and later a series of strokes. He divorced his wife, left his family, and eventually ended up on the streets, unable to function or work.

Like many who become homeless, Vince fell out of the seven systems that were created to help you and me—education, health care, mental health, employment, housing, family, and even religion. Falling out of one or two of these systems may be reversible, but falling out of most or all of them can lead to insurmountable challenges and a downward spiral that ends on the streets.

While on the streets, Vince struggled with alcoholism and continued to be belligerent. Whenever police officers stopped him, he invited them to beat him up. If officers smarted off to him, he would just say, "Make my day." They did. But they also began bringing him to Room In The Inn's Guest House, an alternative to incarceration for people picked up for public intoxication, to sober up.

I was both sad and relieved that Vince was back in my community. He made me wonder what might have happened to me and my other Assumption School classmates if we'd been taken out of our supportive, accepting network at an impressionable age. A Room In The Inn volunteer named Don used to say to Vince, "Don't you know people love you? Why don't you believe it? You don't need to be living on the street." Vince finally began to listen, started participating in our overnight winter shelter program and began to find a new community at Room In The Inn. But it was slow going.

For those like Vince who experience homelessness, the invitation to participate in community can be extremely challenging. Many have had failed relationships in every aspect of life—within their families, at school, and on the job. They legitimately wonder, when invited to enter another community, if they are being set up to fail yet again. People who cannot imagine the lives of the unhoused wonder, "Why can't they just get a job? There are plenty of jobs out there." Yet the obstacles the unhoused face require so much courage and determination from them that they often give up, resigned and hopeless. This can be mistaken, on the surface, as "choosing" their lifestyle. When failure is so prevalent in their past, success is difficult to imagine.

More than anything, Room In The Inn strives to create a community for the most vulnerable that never rejects them, no matter what. We try to model relationships among staff and volunteers in such a way that those who are homeless actually enjoy being on Room In The Inn's campus. When they feel our warm hospitality welcoming them, they can begin again to feel what it means to belong.

Sometimes, people return to Room In The Inn not simply for services, but to say "hello" or to tell us that they do not feel they belong anywhere else. Congregations that partner with Room In The Inn to provide shelter and food over the winter months are also vital in providing the unhoused with a sense of belonging.

Over the years, I've described the program as a sanctuary from the violence of the streets, Ellis Island for urban refugees, a Red Cross tent in a war zone, an oasis in an asphalt desert, a gathering of friends, and a rewriting of the original "no room in the inn" story from St. Luke's gospel recounting the birth of Christ.

I've come to realize, though, that the most important image I've used is of the communion meal.

Consider all the ways we eat a meal—often on the run. Twelve people sitting individually at a McDonald's are each eating a meal. But something is missing. The gathering of twelve people at a Room In The Inn congregation also experience a meal, to be sure, but something more.

A communion meal involves sharing and intimacy. It reaches the depths of the soul and the heights of mystery. It is called sacred by people of religious faith. Yet unlike the sacredness of God, no one ever doubts or needs to prove its existence. A communion meal is experienced the way we experience sunsets and mountain tops.

For decades at Room In The Inn, both unhoused and housed people have gathered to share such a meal. Reluctantly at first, for suspicions were plenty. Some congregation members stood on the other side of a serving counter, like human vending machines dispensing food without sharing, while homeless guests went off to eat in a corner by themselves.

But God's invitation to come, sit down, and eat together ultimately won the hearts of all. And the miracle of a communion meal was born.

Regardless of the food—chili, lasagna, hamburger, potatoes, corn, salad, rolls, and drink—a Room In The Inn meal carries the force of the unleavened bread, the unblemished lamb and choicest wine eaten and drunk at those ancient Passover suppers and at the Last Supper.

I believe it remains our most important connection. Room In The Inn may be safe and warm, clean and quiet, dependable and secure. But most importantly, it is loving hospitality—found in the sharing, the laughter, the tears, the memories, the hopes, and all those other moments that bring us into communion with each other and with God.

> Blessed are those who break bread together,
> for they shall find God in their midst.

Over time, Vince was drawn into many communion meals at Room In The Inn. He developed relationships with staff members and others like himself who were experiencing homelessness. They started to look out for him and watch over him. When he didn't show up as expected, people on the streets started asking, "How's Vince? Have you heard from him today?"

One day, Vince said to me, "Charlie, it's really funny how things work out. When I was a boy, my mother wanted me to become a priest, and look what happened. You became a priest and I became a wino." I responded, "Everybody's got to be something!" Vince wore my words like a badge. He repeated our conversation over and over to others. All agreed that he really was something. Something special. Someone worthy of love, as are we all.

Like most unhoused people, Vince did not live long. The crisis of homelessness is the crisis of death. The life expectancy of those living on our streets is between the ages of forty-eight and fifty-two, about twenty years less than the lifespan most of us will live. Vince's days were shortened because he was dealing with the aftereffects not only of a brain injury and strokes, but also alcoholism. Vince died on October 13, 1990. He was forty-nine years old. I gave his funeral homily. *We're on this earth to get ready to die.*

Then we hung the portrait of my lifelong friend and me in our boardroom in a place of honor.

After Vince passed away, his son came to visit me. He said to me, "I never knew my father, and I want to know him before I die." I toured Vince's son around, told him stories, and shared with him Vince's daily activities while at Room In The Inn.

As I talked with Vince's son, I realized Vince left a lot of good in this world despite his hard life. The time we spent together was a redemption moment. A Beatitude Moment.

> Blessed are those who rarely find love in their lives. They must not be abandoned.

⚔ 29 ⚔

The Man in the Morgue

> Whatever you do for one of the least of these brothers and sisters of mine, you do for me.
>
> —MATTHEW 25:40

ONCE, DURING THE YEARS WHEN I WAS THE PASTOR AT HOLY NAME, the telephone rang in the middle of the night. I was dead asleep and fumbled around to answer it. I remember checking my clock. It was around 3 a.m., never a good sign.

I answered, "Hello, hello?"

A voice on the other end asked, "Are you a priest?"

I said, "Yes, I am. How can I help you?"

The voice said, "I want to kill myself."

Suddenly, I was wide awake, as charged as a bolt of lightning. I asked, "Where are you?"

The voice said, "I'm at Mapco."

I said, "You're not far from here. Can you come over?"

"Yes," the voice said.

I responded, "I'm putting on some coffee. Come on over and we'll talk. I'll have coffee ready for you when you get here."

The voice said, "I'll be there."

I went downstairs. I made a pot of coffee and waited to see if the voice would make an appearance.

Soon I heard the doorbell. I opened the door and saw a man. I didn't recognize him. He was a stranger. He was very ordinary looking—a White man of medium build with dark hair, probably in his forties. We went to the kitchen and sat down to drink some coffee and talk.

I told him my name. He did not tell me his.

I said, "How can I help you?"

He said, "I don't want to live anymore."

In the back of my mind, I remembered conversations from my years in seminary about how to help someone in distress. We were taught to ask a series of questions to encourage the person to talk about something important in their life.

Psychologist Rollo May has written, "Depression is the inability to wish." In other words, it is the inability to want, to yearn, to seek, to desire, to construct a future. I recalled this theory from the classroom as I sat there, holding a coffee cup. I knew I needed to ask enough questions to find something this man loved, hoped for, or desired.

I said, "Please tell me what is going on." He said nothing.

I asked, "Are you married?"

"No."

"Do you have any children?"

"No."

"Do you have parents?"

"No."

"Do you have a brother or sister?"

"No."

"A cousin, aunt, or uncle?"

"No."

"Do you have any family at all?"

"No."

"Do you have friends?"

"No."

"Do you have any plans?"

"No."

"Do you have any money?"

"No."

"Do you have a place to live?"

"No."

Each time the answer came back negative. He had no relationships, no support, no plans. Repeatedly, he offered nothing but a one-word response to my questions: no. I seemed close to exhausting the questions that might lead him to some desire to live.

Then I asked, "Tell me, are you working?"

He said, "No, I lost my job."

"Where did you work?"

"I worked at the morgue."

"Tell me about that. What did you do there?"

He said, "I cleaned up the morgue."

I said, "Tell me what that means. What exactly did you do?"

He began to speak as if he was still working there. He described hosing down metal tables and cleaning up after bodies were brought in and autopsied. He said, "The morgue is a gruesome place. When doctors come to the morgue, they sometimes make light of the experience. But I try to keep it as clean as I possibly can."

I asked, "How do you do that?"

He said, "I try to treat each piece with the utmost respect."

I repeated what he said as a question: "You try to treat each piece of flesh with the utmost respect?"

"Yes." That's all he said.

There was silence. I was stunned. I couldn't believe what I'd just heard. This man had nothing at all. Yet, he was able to articulate the meaning of life as he saw it.

All my questions were useless. There was nothing I could say to him that was more powerful than what he said to me. "I try to treat each piece with the utmost respect."

I said, "I don't know your name. When you leave here tonight, I don't know where you're going. But let me tell you—what you've said is something I'll never forget.

"I don't know what you're going to do tomorrow. I would like for you to come back so we can talk some more. But whatever happens and whatever you decide to do, I'll never forget you as long as I live.

Marquis Churchwell contemplates the Memorial Tree in Room In The Inn's lobby, with its leaves bearing the names of guests who have died. A few months after this photo was taken, Marquis would be killed in a senseless act of violence. His name is now part of the tree.

The name of one of Room In The Inn's first guests, Michael "Bear" Hodges, on a leaf of the Memorial Tree.

"I want you to know how good you are. Do you realize how good you are?"

He said not a word. I had nothing left to say.

I couldn't give him the help he was seeking. Yet he gave me a message I needed to hear. He tried to treat the least of what God has made, lifeless flesh, with the utmost respect.

With that, we exchanged a few pleasantries. I wanted him to stay. I told him he was loved.

I remember thinking that I always wanted to know my father better—my father whose eyes I saw wide open as he lay on a bed in a mortuary when I was only four years old. My father, whose eyes my Aunt Mary walked over and closed so tenderly, treating him with the utmost respect.

I remember thinking that I wanted to know the Man in the Morgue better. But he was ready to go. He stood up. I showed him to the door. He left, and I never saw or heard from him again.

I never forgot him.

What a gift to be the one who treats everything God has made with the utmost respect, without exception. That's what the world is missing.

> Blessed are those who feel no hope, for they shall know love and everlasting life.

EDITORS' NOTE: *One question among many that Charlie asked The Man in the Morgue was, "Do you know how good you are?" He asked this same question of everyone he met, his way of reminding them they were worthy of love—and remembrance.*

⚡ 30 ⚡

The Chaplain

EDITORS' NOTE: *One of Charlie's favorite stories was a baseball story—specifically, the game he witnessed on July 18, 1999. Charlie told the magical tale the rest of his life. We've asked several of his friends, relations, and fellow baseball fanatics to recount what they heard, time and again, about The Perfect Game.**

Charles and I were both New York Yankees fans because The Yankees were Daddy's team. Whoever your father roots for, that's who you root for.

He and I were very, very close growing up. We did everything together, including playing sports. Baseball was our favorite. He was one of those guys who wanted to be on the field. He wanted to play.

I remember once his team found itself going into a game without a catcher, and the coach asked if anyone had catching experience. Charles said, "Yeah, I do, I do!" Well, he'd never caught in his life! He got ready to start playing the position, and the umpire said, "Hey, buddy, don't you wear shin guards?" The umpire had to pause the

Charlie at the bat.

---

* A perfect game is one in which a pitcher completes a minimum of nine innings with no batter from the opposing team reaching base. As of 2023, only twenty-four perfect games have been pitched in the history of Major League Baseball.

game for a minute so Charles could figure out how to suit up.

He just loved to play. He didn't ever sit anything out.

—*Jerry Strobel, Charles's older brother*

I got a phone call from Charlie on July 18, 1999, asking, "Do you know where I am?" I replied, "No, where are you?" Charlie said, "I am standing in right field at Yankee Stadium walking over to the monuments in center field." I asked if he was going to a game. He said he was going to be the chaplain for the game that day. Someone from the archdiocese in New York knew he was a Yankees fan and asked if he wanted to be the guest chaplain. Of course, he said yes!

—*Lenny Frenette, Charlie's teammate in adult amateur leagues*

The day of the game coincided with Yogi Berra Day.* Yogi Berra was at Yankee Stadium for the first time in fourteen years. He'd stayed away all that time due to a conflict with Yankees owner George Steinbrenner. That day also brought many of Yogi's former teammates to the stadium, including Don Larsen who threw out the first pitch to Yogi. Larsen and Berra had been the battery [pitcher and catcher] for Larsen's perfect game. Larsen pitched a perfect game in 1956, the first for the Yankees and the only perfect game ever in the World Series. It was a game Charlie surely listened to on the family Motorola when he was a boy.

—*Rachel Hester, Executive Director of Room In The Inn*

What came next was extraordinary, particularly because the battery from 1956 was there to witness it. David Cone was on the mound for the Yankees that day. History was about to be made and Charles was there for it. Not only was he there, he was on the field beforehand, he was in the dugout, he was leading the team in prayer.

He was able to talk to Yankee players. He wanted to talk to Paul O'Neill, who had played in Nashville for the Nashville Sounds. O'Neill was getting his bats in shape for the game, and Charles tried to approach him for some Nashville small talk. But he was told by the chaplain who'd invited him that the players were preparing mentally and logistically for the game and not to bother them.

—*Richard Courtney, husband of Charles's niece Beth Courtney and a diehard Atlanta Braves fan*

---

* Yogi Berra (1925-2015) was one of the greatest catchers in baseball history and won ten World Series championships, the most of any MLB player. He was also a manager and coach.

Charlie with longtime teammate Lenny Frenette.

I watched the game later that day. What I thought might be a no-hitter ended up being a perfect game! I was so happy for Charlie, knowing he was there, and on Yogi Berra Day of all days. He was one of Charlie's favorite players!

—Lenny Frenette

One thing that increased the drama was that there was a rain delay in the third inning. It was a thirty-three-minute rain delay, and Charles was worried David Cone would not come back to pitch. But Yankee manager Joe Torre went with Cone after the delay.

—Richard Courtney

Later, Charlie would reflect on the crowd, the excitement, being in the dugout, the anticipation as the momentum continued after a long rain delay. He talked about one of his old friends from Nashville, Chuck Meriweather, who was also a Father Ryan High School graduate, being the third-base umpire that day.

I wish I loved baseball the way he did. He would continually remind me how rare the experience had been. Only sixteen perfect games in MLB history and two for the Yankees before July 18, 1999. As Charlie told the story, it was as if all the baseball stars were aligned that day and he got to be among them.

—Rachel Hester

A couple days later, Charlie told me all about it. He said the players were "huge"—that they all looked like Greek gods! He clearly brought them all good luck that day.

—Lenny Frenette

Every time Charles told the story, he was filled with wonder, like he still couldn't believe it had happened and he had been part of it. A rain-delayed perfect game on Yogi Berra day in Yankee Stadium, witnessed from the owner's box and complete with a trip to the clubhouse for pregame. Perfect in every way.

—Richard Courtney

The last summer of his life, he wasn't following baseball as closely as he normally did, so in our phone calls and visits, I often reported highlights to him. One of those was the Yankee's Domingo Germán's perfect game against the Oakland A's on June 28, 2023. And off he went. "Did I tell you about the time I saw David Cone pitch a perfect game at Yankee Stadium on Yogi Berra Day?" And I said, "Yes, about a million times." I told him it was one of his many "longest stories ever told." We both laughed. I told him that Germán had thrown only ninety-nine pitches. And then we both simultaneously said, "But the A's got twenty-seven outs!" a reference to something we often pointed to in baseball for sure, but also as a comment on baseball and life's chances—both teams are guaranteed twenty-seven outs.

—Kay West, *a writer who once covered the Yankees and was Charlie's longtime friend*

He always recounted the story with humility, as if he'd been given a gift. I remember once, he mentioned that by the seventh inning he was watching from Steinbrenner's box. I perked up and said, "Did I hear that right? You were in the owner's box?" I wondered how I had missed that detail before. It occurred to me that I might have missed it because he didn't emphasize that part. The owner's box wasn't as important to him as the magic on the field.

Charlie loved baseball more than any other sport. He loved the fact that the game isn't run on a clock. There are twenty-seven outs, no matter how long it takes, and you're always safe at home. He saw it as a great metaphor for our work at Room In The Inn, too. In the end, it was a great metaphor for his own life.

—*Rachel Hester*

When I think of Charlie in the next life, I think often of the scene in *Field of Dreams* where a long-deceased baseball player, glove in hand, walks out from between stalks of corn onto a gorgeous, lush, impossibly green ball field and asks, "Is this heaven?" I can see Charlie saying the same, and then asking, "Did I tell you about the time I saw David Cone pitch a perfect game?"

—*Kay West*

CHARLIE STROBEL'S BASEBALL PRAYER: Oh, God—divine umpire in the sky—forgive the error of our ways and help us to arrive safely home. Amen.

He wasn't perfect, but his life was a perfect game.
—Rachel Hester

Charlie's favorite New York Yankees shirt hangs in the dugout of First Horizon Park during the citywide gathering on August 11, 2023, to celebrate his life.

EDITORS' NOTE: *On August 11, 2023, five days after Charles Strobel died, Room In The Inn hosted a citywide gathering at First Horizon Park to celebrate his life. Home of Charlie's beloved Nashville Sounds Baseball Club, First Horizon is located on the site of the Old Sulphur Dell ballfield that lit up his childhood and ignited his love of the game.*

There were no givers or receivers among more than 1,500 people who came to say goodbye that day, nor among the tens of thousands from far and wide who watched online. It was a gathering of family, the kind you are born into and the kind you choose. The housed and unhoused sat together in the stands. Status, circumstances, titles, and religious denomination meant nothing. Everyone celebrated and sang, in unison and in gratitude, for a life lived joyfully for others.

Through it all, Charlie's smiling face lit up the guitar-shaped scoreboard in the outfield, shining down on the community he loved and served so well.

Room In The Inn resident Jerry Lewis signing the guest book before Charlie's celebration of life.

A choir of Charles's great-nieces and great-nephews, who performed at his celebration of life, pose beneath a photo of his smiling face. It dominated First Horizon Park's signature guitar-shaped scoreboard throughout the gathering.

Guests at the gathering join together to recite The Lord's Prayer, which is said each evening during Room In The Inn's winter shelter program.

EPILOGUE
Pick Up the Burden

WE ARE ALL POOR and we are all worthy of love.

I believe I was born to live this truth every day of my life. I believe we are all born to do the same. If we're on this earth to get ready to die, as Father Dan said, then this is how we get ready: recognize our common poverty, recognize our common goodness—and act accordingly.

I have tried to act by alleviating the suffering of people who suffer the most—the poorest of the poor, those who have fallen out of the seven systems society creates to support its members: education, health care, mental health care, employment, housing, family, and, in many cases, organized religion.

As I come to the end of my life and reflect, I am aware that the number of people who are destitute and suffering is growing. In fact, we seem to be experiencing the injustice of socioeconomic inequality more acutely these days than at any time I can recall.

Yet I have hope for the future. Why? Because I believe in you. If you are reading these words and have come this far with me, I believe you can and will go farther—that you will pick up the burden and carry on.

I want to leave you with a few things to think about as you go forward.

The first is this:

We live in a world where both grace and tragedy coexist. This creates a lingering dissatisfaction. One spiritual writer calls it "a divine discontent."

What is this divine discontent? It's the part of the Jesus story that lives in us.

Jesus was a first-century itinerant Jewish rabbi, or preacher, who was willing to step outside the social conventions of his day and speak up for the poor and marginalized in the face of an oppressive, brutal political regime and highly structured religious authority. Jesus ultimately died as a criminal of the state despite doing nothing wrong.

The Jesus story culminates at the Last Supper the night before he dies, when he shares the Passover meal, washes the feet of his disciples, and asks them to do the same. The Jesus story is our story to absorb into our hearts and appropriate into our lives—to act on the words, "Love one another as I have loved you."

Divine discontent lives in us whenever we yearn for this kind of love, whenever we imagine a world without war, a nation without poverty, a city without homelessness, a family without abuse, children without empty stomachs, and an economic system without greed. The notion that injustices in our world must be addressed is proven because of the discontent that resides inside of us. It's a reflection of yearning for the divine. We look at our world and we're not happy with what we see.

We should be grateful we are created this way. We should take heart that we can imagine a better life for everyone. For when we do, God's divine story becomes more and more a part of us. This discontent is grace. It carries us on the journey as we help others along the way.

We move through life with grace when we see our own stories as part of a divine story rather than just a series of disconnected events. God's story forms us as a community symbolized by the eating of a meal—not just any meal, a communion meal. Around a communion table, we give and receive food that satisfies all our hungers.

You will enjoy a wealth of communion meals in the days to come if you do so in the spirit of connection rather than correction. I served many a supper in remembrance of Mrs. Hopwood, who showed me by example that Doy was not my problem to solve but my brother to love. I gathered at many a table in remembrance of Mama, who taught me how to "put the big pot in the little pot." I urge you to offer up your own communion meals in remembrance of those who were or are examples to you of our divine connection to one another.

God's story is not about individuals, it's about the kingdom of justice and peace. Take heart that if you do work that is for peace, you will be in

Guests of Room In The Inn, who traveled in buses to First Horizon Park with a police escort, make their way into the stadium for Charlie's celebration of life.

communion. And if you are in communion, you will be at peace, even in the presence of divine discontent.

Now, to the work of peace—the second thing I want to share:

We are in a new millennium and a new world is being born. The old world is dying all around us. Karl Barth, considered by many as the greatest Protestant theologian of the twentieth century, wrote that societies sometimes experience in their history a "time between times." A time between times brings with it deep anxiety, extravagant dreaming, and depressing pessimism.

We find ourselves in a time between times today. As our old familiar values dissolve in the face of technology, we are witnessing increased incidences of a whole list of problems: vice, crime, mental illness, suicide, drugs and addiction, broken and dysfunctional homes, child abuse, racism, violence, murder, war, and despair. In a time between times, it's natural to take refuge in what we know and attribute dark purposes to what we don't know. In a time between times, we find ourselves acting out of our insecurities and fears.

But such a time requires exactly the opposite of us. It requires courage. We must become part of a bridge to a new world order. We can start by recognizing our shared poverty—our shared identity as *the anawim.* Look into the face of one poor person and see in that person the whole world of global economic injustice, racism, classism, inequality, terrorism, and war. This world is hungry and homeless and poor, and it is waiting for our grace.

Most of us assume we are insignificant in the swirl of historical forces. Our culture reinforces our feelings of impotence. An excessive availability of commercial entertainment soaks up our time and our surplus wealth when it could be better spent on building community and transforming society.

Millions of people have the potential to be leaders and visionaries, but most are modest and given to self-deprecation, much like Moses and Jeremiah when they were first called to act as leaders. Who, me?

But if not you, then who?

I believe 2,000 years of Judeo-Christian history provide you with a framework for action today—and it is contained in the meaning of *anawim*, summarized in the phrase, *"God's preferential option for the poor."* I have found *anawim* is consistent with similar teachings from all the major religions of the world, and can be expressed in the following six principles that have become universally recognized priorities in social justice teaching; one need not be a person of faith to accept them:

- The needs of the poor take priority over the wants of the rich.
- The freedom of the dominated takes priority over the liberty of the powerful.
- The participation of marginalized groups takes priority over the preservation of systems that exclude them.
- The rights of workers take priority over the maximization of profits.
- The preservation of the environment takes priority over uncontrolled industrial expansion.
- The production to meet social needs takes priority over the production for military purposes.*

To these six I have added a seventh:

- The sanctification of sexuality forbids sexual abuse.

The modern world has paid a heavy price for shunting aside the principles

---

* "God's preferential option for the poor" is one of the major tenets of twentieth-century social justice teaching; its principles have been widely adopted and adapted by many faiths. Charlie relied on and circulated a list of six he had read in the National Catholic Reporter, a leading Catholic newspaper, in the 1970s.

of *anawim*. We have glorified war and deregulated greed, and now have a social fabric that is threatening to completely unravel in this time between times. But, to paraphrase Charles Dickens, the worst of times often are inextricably linked with the best of times. All who care about social justice have an opportunity to resurrect *anawim* and make it a guiding force in our world.

I offer to you these principles as a direction, a path ahead into your future—pillars supporting the bridge each of you can help build to attain justice for the poor.

You can use this time between times to upend society's dependence on material wealth as a sign of communal health—and our reliance on war and violence to defend our possessions—and begin to create a society that values the peace, security, and happiness of all people. I believe you will do it.

Finally, I leave you with this:

Several years ago, I had an opportunity to hear the Dalai Lama in New York. Among the many things he said, I remember three.

1. Altruism is the attitude of freeing others from suffering.
2. Compassion is the attitude of shifting our focus from my suffering to the suffering of others.
3. The greater the sense of connection we have, the more unable we are to bear the suffering of another.

William Boyd was one of several residents of Room In The Inn who helped host the gathering by manning tables filled with water bottles, memorial cards, "Love Your Neighbor, Y'all" fans, programs, and guest books.

Over the years, I've heard people speak about how hard it is to bear another person's suffering, whether visiting a friend in a hospital or consoling someone in grief.

The Dalai Lama's words acknowledge that our connections to others can break our hearts. This may be why we often isolate and anesthetize ourselves with our surplus wealth and excessive entertainment.

But if we follow his logic, and we must, he is telling us gently that we have no choice but to relieve the suffering of others. Despite the pain, we must. This is what makes us human. And this is why, I believe, we must focus first on the faces of the poor, the disenfranchised, and the homeless of our world. For they remain the lowest and the least in the strata of every nation and every culture. And they have suffered enough.

Yet there is also joy in taking up a small part of someone else's burden, the part you can manage—the part you think you can carry. You will be strengthened by it and in turn you will know that someone else will not be crushed by what they cannot manage alone. This balance between people is the essence of love and of joy.

This balance makes the burden light.

I urge you to join with others to pick it up, which will make the burden even lighter. You can do it by connecting your own stories—your own Beatitude Moments—with the stories of the poor and transforming them into a new, collective vision of justice for all people.

Realizing a vision that embraces our shared poverty and lifts everyone out of needless suffering will require imagination. But I trust that you can summon it.

If enough of you commit to operate within a societal framework rooted in and guided by an understanding of *anawim*, you will slowly but surely realize a world in which the needs of the poor become the priorities of all. You will help initiate a groundswell that substitutes a societal and economic model driven by greed and selfishness for one that is guided by a moral imperative rooted in love of neighbor.

All the great religions of the world remind us that we are called by God to be one family.

The Dalai Lama says, "All six billion of us are one." Jesus said, when gifting us with the Beatitudes, "Blessed are the poor." The Hebrew translation is, "Blessed are the *anawim*."

Charlie kneeling by Lake Louise in Banff National Park while visiting Calgary, Canada, in 1997 for the opening of a Room In The Inn program.

The message for our time and for all time is, "Blessed are all of us."
Please remember how good you are. Then carry one another. And carry on.

                                              I love you,

                                                          —C. S.

ACKNOWLEDGMENTS

FROM THE TIME HE WAS A SMALL CHILD until his last days, Charles Strobel welcomed people in. He wrote *The Kingdom of the Poor* the way he lived his life. He invited every person who walked through his door to read with him, talk with him, and share their thoughts about his "simple stories, each one a story of God."

Charlie also had a gift for gratitude. His mother always told him, "People don't have to be nice to you," and he took this to heart, deeply appreciative of every kindness. If he were here to thank the many people who made his memoir possible, he'd have compiled a list as long as the book itself.

But he is not. We are left to do our best without him. We apologize to anyone we have failed to acknowledge. Please know he wouldn't have forgotten—and he would ask you to forgive us!

With that said and on Charlie's behalf, we are thankful for:

- Ann Patchett, who first encouraged Charlie to write a memoir and has championed his story like no other;
- Betsy Phillips, who believed in *The Kingdom of the Poor* from the beginning; and all her colleagues at Vanderbilt University Press, who moved mountains to bring it to the page in record time;
- Monsignor Owen Campion, Richard Courtney, Alice Strobel Eadler, Lenny Frenette, Rachel Hester, Becca Stevens, Jerry Strobel, Pat Thompson, and Kay West, whose memories of Charlie added depth and perspective to his own;

- everyone who read the manuscript and offered their thoughts;

- the caregivers from Touching Hearts and Mary, Queen of Angels, who attended to Charlie's every need and heard his every word; his doctors and nurses, who always gave him their very best; and Beth Courtney, Alice Eadler, and Martin Strobel, who made such exquisite care possible.

- The Wednesday Breakfast Club, aka "The Mystic Knights," who helped Charlie solve all the problems of the world and saw their friend through thick and thin;

- the *Anawim* prayer group, with whom he dove into The Mystery;

- the baseball lovers in Charlie's life, who took the field with him, traded stats with him, and marveled with him at the magic of the game;

- the justice-seekers in Charlie's life, who made sure the road he walked toward a better world was never lonely;

- the priests of the Nashville Diocese, with whom he served his Nashville Catholic family; and the leaders of religious denominations across Nashville and beyond, with whom he served people of all faiths;

- the Father Ryan High School class of 1961, who first nicknamed him "Sunshine";

- Assumption Parish and Germantown, the original kingdoms of justice and peace that helped make Charlie who he was;

- the staff, counselors and campers at Camp Marymount, one of his favorite places on the planet;

- Madeleine DeMoss and her family, who loved Charlie like their own;

- Charlie's many relatives—from his first cousins through his fiftieth—every one of whom he was so proud to claim;

- his nieces and nephews, to whom he was a second father; and his great-nieces and great-nephews, to whom he was a second grandfather;

- his brother-in-law Bob Eadler, who answered every call at every hour of the day or night with the words, "I'll be there";

- and again, his brother Jerry and his sister Alice. Along with Veronica, who died in 2022, they were his first friends, last friends, and best friends.

✣ Charles would also want us to mention his brother-in-law Tom Seigenthaler, who died in 2004, and his sister-in-law Pat Holzapfel Strobel, who died in 2021. He dearly loved them both.

✣ Finally, his beloved community:

the faith-filled parishioners of Holy Name Catholic Church, who were the first to move out from behind the serving line and into communion;

members of the staff and board of directors at Room In The Inn, who pick up the burden daily with purpose, creativity and devotion;

every Room In The Inn volunteer, congregation, and supporter, who are the heart and soul of a program that depends on selfless service;

and most especially, the people of the kingdom Charlie sought and the kingdom he built—the guests of Room In The Inn.

He wrote this book for you.

Katie Seigenthaler and Amy Frogge
May 2024

APPENDIX A

Charles Strobel's Eulogy for His Mother, Mary Catherine Strobel

MAMA ALWAYS WANTED A BIG FUNERAL; she loved them so, and hoped that when her time came, everyone would know about it. Once again, things seem to go her way. Once again, she has us laughing and crying at the same time.

In Shakespeare's play *Antony and Cleopatra*, Cleopatra says to Antony as he dies, with all of the anguish and heartache in her soul:

> Noblest of men, would you die? Have you no care of me?
> Shall I live in this dull world, which in your absence is no
> better than a sty?

Until early Thursday morning, none of us—Veronica, Jerry, Alice, or me—knew how painfully empty Mama must have felt when Daddy died thirty-nine years ago, December 21, 1947. In her eyes and in the eyes of those who knew him, he was the noblest of men, her source of life and love.

When Daddy died, she gathered us together and kneeling around his bed, said, "God is going to help us, your Daddy will always be there to watch over us, and we need to stay together." Then we said the rosary.

Two days later, after the family had returned from the cemetery to our house down the street at 1212, to relax and unwind, a call came from a woman whose friend had a little baby who was dying. She needed Mama. So Mama left her house full of company, her children, her own grief, and went to the woman and child. She stayed with the mother and baptized the child. Later the child died.

I think it's important to understand that in the handling of the events of my Daddy's death, Mama was teaching us a lesson for us to learn today. And that lesson has two parts.

The first part is this:

As devastating and as empty as her death is to us—and it is the hardest thing we have ever done—we must paraphrase her words. "God is going to help us, our Mama will always be there to watch over us, and we need to stay together."

The second lesson is this:

Now two days later, as we return to our homes, there will still be great, great needs all around us, and we must try to respond to them as she would want us to. "It can be done," she says. "It must be done," she says.

Many have said that she did not deserve to die the way that she did. Yet for years, we have heard it said that "God did not spare his only Son but delivered him up, and the Son emptied himself and humbled himself, obediently accepting even death, death on a cross." In Mama's death, our family believes that the viciousness inflicted on such gentleness and kindness, as was her way, brings about a great *communion* with Jesus.

So, how can we question its course? It seems to run true to the form of Jesus's own death. And why speak of anger and revenge? Those words are not compatible with the very thought of our Mother.

So, I say to everyone: We are not angry or vengeful, just deeply hurt. And you and many others have helped to ease our pain.

We know the answers are not easy and clear. But we still believe in the miracle of forgiveness . . . and extend our arms in that embrace.

APPENDIX B

Strobel Family Statement after the Murder of Mary Catherine Strobel

TODAY OUR FAMILY IS GRIEVING deeply over the death of our mother. This terrible event in our lives points out how heartless our world can be. But our mother spent her whole life working to change that. She gave us lessons every day about what gentleness and kindness can mean in even the most forgotten lives. She loved people of all races, especially the poor, and was our inspiration.

Perhaps, it is the irony of God that a woman who abhorred violence died so violently, that a woman who gave so much to the needy lost her life in the act of serving them.

No horror can change our belief that the concern and love that our mother meant to us and to so many others is the best response to the violence and disregard we see around us all in the world.

The circumstances of our mother's death, we know, will bring the attention of many people. We will remember forever the sympathy and friendship expressed by so many; but most of all, we hope that our mother's memory will be in terms of how she lived for others. If this community on this occasion can be reminded of that and can renew itself to a concern for the troubled and the distressed, then we know that our mother would smile.

APPENDIX C

Charles Strobel's Statement in Opposition to the Death Penalty for William Scott Day

AS A FAMILY, WE ARE INVOLVED with the community in its search for justice in the killing of our Mother. As with all families of murder victims, it remains a futile search, for no judgment can bring about Mama's return.

Nor can any judgment reverse the events in the life of William Scott Day. Since December 9, 1986, his life has been changed forever.

Now that the judicial system has asked our opinion in the case, I have some thoughts on the matter.

I think that the question before us, as a family, is one of mercy and forgiveness, something that is possible to achieve. We claim no higher authority than Jesus and make no greater appeal than his words: "You have heard it said, 'An eye for an eye and a tooth for a tooth.' But what I say to you is love your enemies, do good to those who persecute you. If a person strikes you on the right cheek, turn and offer him the other."

I believe that we need to petition the district attorney not to seek the death penalty for William Scott Day, accused of murdering our Mother. I believe we need to say, "Spare his life." Enough is enough. I can think of no way that his execution would bring us satisfaction.

Besides the appeal we make in this community for his life, I think that we believe in one another as members of a family that has been taught from our ancestors the beauty and value of human life. We now inherit that tradition and want to pass it on to our children and to their children and to their children. I hope that ages from now our family descendants will look back at our actions and understand that in an age of vengeance, we chose not to be vengeful but tried to be faithful to our most cherished family teaching, namely, that God is love itself, has given us his life generously, yes, even unto death, and expects nothing less from us.

In my mind, William Scott Day is a child of God, created in the image of God, and loved by God. Can we think of him in any other way? In the destiny of God, he is forever linked to us and has become a part of us and we a part of him.

I believe that our words of forgiveness are only symbolic if we do not use every opportunity within the system to prevent his execution.

Finally, I want the court to give him the maximum number of years for the protection of society.

APPENDIX D

Room In The Inn Rights and Responsibilities

THE WORLD OF THE UNHOUSED is filled with hatred and violence. Everyone at Room In The Inn does whatever we can to create sanctuary. We start by defining violence as four types of abuse: physical, verbal, racial, and sexual.

In our Room In The Inn orientation for guests, volunteers, and staff members, we identify these four types of abuse and establish principles to combat them, each one rooted in respect. These principles exist to secure the individual rights of all participants and to ensure the program runs smoothly—all within an atmosphere free of violence:

All guests have the right to:
- use our services without discrimination
- be safe and to be treated with dignity and respect
- be treated objectively and professionally
- participate in the development of program goals and plans
- confidentiality, except in situations involving criminal activity
- access to a formal grievance process

All guests are responsible for treating others with dignity and respect; and for rejecting violence, threats and intimidation. Unacceptable behavior includes
- physical fighting of any kind

- language that is obscene, vulgar, defamatory, disrespectful, or demeaning
- words and actions that are racist and incite racial tensions
- words or actions that are sexually offensive or abusive toward another

APPENDIX E

Dr. Martin Luther King Jr.'s Principles of Nonviolence

Principle One: Nonviolence is a way of life for courageous people. It is active nonviolent resistance to evil. It is aggressive spiritually, mentally and emotionally.

Principle Two: Nonviolence seeks to win friendship and understanding. The result of nonviolence is redemption and reconciliation. The purpose of nonviolence is the creation of the Beloved Community.

Principle Three: Nonviolence seeks to defeat injustice, not people. Nonviolence recognizes that evildoers are also victims and are not evil people. The nonviolent resister seeks to defeat evil, not people.

Principle Four: Nonviolence holds that suffering can educate and transform. Nonviolence accepts suffering without retaliation. Unearned suffering is redemptive and has tremendous educational and transforming possibilities.

Principle Five: Nonviolence chooses love instead of hate. Nonviolence resists violence of the spirit as well as the body. Nonviolent love is spontaneous, unmotivated, unselfish and creative.

Principle Six: Nonviolence believes that the universe is on the side of justice. The nonviolent resister has deep faith that justice will eventually win. Nonviolence believes that God is a God of justice.*

---

* The King Center in Atlanta, Georgia.

www.ingramcontent.com/pod-product-compliance
Lightning Source LLC
Chambersburg PA
CBHW041604110426
42742CB00043B/3447